I
EVER
LOSE
MY MIND

Aid in Dying with Advanced Dementia

SUSAN MANN FLANDERS

Susan Mann Flanders

Opus
Self-Publishing
WASHINGTON DC

Published though Opus Self-Publishing Services
Located at:
Politics and Prose Bookstore
5015 Connecticut Ave. NW
Washington, D.C. 20008
www.politics-prose.com / / (202) 364-1919

In Memory of My Father

Robert Mann

Contents

If I Ever Lose My Mind

INTRODUCTION

"Sue, if ever lose my mind, I don't want to go on living."

Sitting in a crowded restaurant, surrounded by my mother and siblings all laughing and talking of other things, I heard my father's words with a start. He spoke quietly, as though confiding a secret, one he wanted me to hear, and, as things turned out, to remember.

I have remembered. I've never forgotten that simple, clear desire, and how it turned out to be prophetic, and impossible, and heartbreaking. Considering the last two years of his life, my father, had he been of sound mind, would have chosen to end his life. Had he been of sound mind, he would have figured out how to do it— but he wasn't. He had lost his mind to Alzheimer's.

He was trapped. Trapped in the locked ward of a nursing home, trapped in a single room with a bed, a TV and some silly toys, trapped in diapers, trapped in a wheelchair. Trapped in the confines of a mind now so confused and so limited that he recognized none of the faces that passed by.

I imagined his mind churning with questions and laments: Was that woman my wife? Who is this person coming, showing me pictures of people I don't know? Who is the little brown and white dog coming into my room with some woman? Do I live here? When can I go home? I hurt; I ache; I can't make the right sounds. The person is putting something in my mouth. My bed feels wet. I want to leave. But I could never know, because he could not tell me anything.

During those years, and for some time before my father became ill, I began thinking about some of the choices people make as they age and begin to face death. I am a retired Episcopal priest, and I've learned first-hand in my ministry of the struggles people have with end-of-life decisions. In this country, we have made great progress with advance directives and living wills to ensure that extraordinary measures will not be used to keep the terminally ill alive against their wishes, especially if they are in extreme pain, or have suffered disability and disfigurement. And at this writing, the states of Oregon, Washington, Vermont, Montana and California along with the District of Columbia recognize a right to aid in dying for those of sound mind who wish to end their lives before the worst ravages of their diseases beset them. Other states are considering such legislation as a groundswell of compassion yields up countless articles, books, and even a few movies wrestling with the issue. Thanks to such advocacy organizations as Compassion and Choices—a non-profit organization founded in 2005 in Denver, Colorado, and the main lobbying group for legal and compassionate aid in dying—support is building across the country for more legalization of such measures. Not a week goes by in which I don't read about end-of-life decisions, and how palliative care and aid in dying afford paths to our final ends that are so much more merciful than a desperate, all-out battle against the inevitable—a battle that is often waged in Intensive Care Units far from the comfort of a patient's home and the surrounding love of family and friends.

I am encouraged by this progress. When I was growing up, money, sex, and death were all avoided in polite conversation, even though people probably think about these three things more than about almost any others. Even today, some people are still reluctant to talk about death, as if it were impolite, simply not done. But now, more and more, folks are willing to discuss their fears, worries and hopes about the end of life more openly.

What I don't read much about at all seems to be a dark, almost taboo region in all these conversations about the end of life: that is the question of aid in dying for victims of dementia. Most of what I read is about people who are mentally competent and thus able to be present and clear in their own end-of-life decisions. But what about those who are certain before their illness takes hold that they would never want to live out their final days under the terrible effects of Alzheimer's or other dementia?

Of all people who would not want to live out the final days of a horrifying illness, I believe that it is these Alzheimer's and dementia patients who would most want and most benefit from the option of assisted suicide. But they, more than physical sufferers with mental competency, would need help. Once the all-but-frail threads of their humanity had worn away, once they were no longer really persons in any sense that would have been meaningful for them, once they had become people they would never, ever have wanted to be, I believe many would choose a swift and painless exit from a life that they would have considered intolerable while they were still mentally competent. It seems to me that the same compassion extended to those with terminal disease who are of sound mind and wish to shorten their lives to avoid severe pain and humiliating debilitation, and are increasingly given the legal option to do so, should also be offered to those suffering extreme dementia, based on their clearly expressed desires and intentions while still of sound mind.

But as yet, the demented who would not want to continue their lives are out of bounds for help in ending their lives. In many of these cases, not just weeks but often months or years of life that is not real human life and personhood could be foregone. This compassionate decision would lessen the terrible fear of late-stage dementia shared by patients and their caregivers alike, give more control over how these long stories end to those who must live them, and conserve resources of money and caring that can severely diminish the lives of all concerned.

These lives can be even further diminished, and unnecessary costs incurred, by the use of antipsychotic drugs as sedatives to calm and control dementia patients in nursing homes. The journalist Hannah Flamm recently described this practice, a not very well-kept secret, in an opinion article in *The Washington Post*. Flamm argues that people should be able to opt out of this kind of "care" which further dehumanizes them, destroys dignity and autonomy (whatever is left of it) and adds to the cost of care. Informed consent by the patient for these medications is a joke, and advance directives ought to specify whether the patient would want them to be used. Further, family members who might make such decisions are often unaware of how these medications are used, and might somehow feel they are helpful to the patient rather than primarily to the staff.

And so, long before my father showed any symptoms of dementia, his words about losing his mind lodged in the recesses of my heart. They haunted me terribly all through his six-year passage through Alzheimer's. They echo in my heart to this day. His words made sense; they were so true to the highly rational, clear thinking man that he was. I heard them back then, and I tucked them away into what I thought might be some distant future scenario. That scenario began to unfold in 1997 when Dad began to show the first hints of mental decline.

I want now to tell his story, the story of who Robert Mann was and how he did lose his mind. I want to tell how it was for him, and for his family, and how it might have been. And, along the way, I want to tell the stories of others afflicted with dementia and how it was for them and their families, and how it might have been different. Because of my father's words, I have never stopped wondering what my mother and siblings and I could have done to honor his words. Because of them, I still question what I might do now to honor them, perhaps by helping others facing their own sad journeys into and through the abyss which dementia opens— opens, but only slowly, too slowly, closes. And I want to look, really look, at what it means to end one's life, with or without help, through the stories of others who have made this choice and through the eyes of those who care for and counsel them.

In the years between my father's comment about losing his mind and his diagnosis of Alzheimer's, I encountered some other stories of people who chose suicide as their lives neared an end, who were able to act on their own wishes and make their own choices, and my interest in such end-of-life decisions began to sharpen. I learned the stories of people who were not cognitively impaired, but were facing what they deemed to be an unendurable final slog towards death. I'll call these stories, "signposts," because they alerted me long before my father's illness to the desire that some have to end their own lives, and of the agonizing choices they and their families faced. These stories unfolded up close; they were people I knew well, people I could not judge abstractly from a distance. In their suicides, they showed me a vein of compassion for those who would bear the burden of their declines, and they showed me the struggles of those who loved them to accept what they did. I also recognized in these stories the apparent lack of conversation between those ending their lives and the people who cared about them. These suicides were violent, shocking and painful. They contrast with the growing number of deaths in some states and countries where people can ask for and legally receive help in dying. That help is non-violent, relatively painless, and usually allows loved ones to share in the decision and be present when death comes. I completely support aid-in-dying legislation for those who choose it, and am encouraged to see more and more states consider it as organizations such as Compassion & Choices press on with their advocacy programs.

Through these stories, and as I've grappled with the problem of end-of-life help for those with dementia, complicated moral questions continue to surface. I am convinced that our society will need to come to terms with them in ways that are legal and caring for all concerned. I realize that there is an array of people who are involved in the choices we make about ending our lives—family members and friends, physicians, sometimes clergy and lawyers—and each of these may have their own perspectives about these choices. Often these views conflict. There are no easy formulas, no "one size fits all' answer, but the steadily increasing number of people with Alzheimer's or other dementias, and their increasing financial and other burdens on our society, demand our attention and compassion.

I will look at the issues through the eyes of a variety of folks whose end-of-life choices   show us the depth of thinking and feeling that surround the prospect of advanced dementia. Based on conversations and interviews, I offer here the narratives that have shaped my heart and my thinking, not only about how things could have been so much better for my father, but for so many others, and perhaps, one day, for myself. Finally, I hope in offering my own experience, I will in some small way be part of the larger ongoing conversation in our country about end-of-life issues and how we can all help each other face death in more compassionate ways.

In the accounts that follow, a number of details and almost all names have been changed, unless otherwise noted, to protect the privacy of the people referenced or interviewed.

ONE

SIGNPOSTS

Long before my father's Alzheimer's prompted my thinking about
difficult end-of-life choices, I was shocked by two suicides, both by
older people who did not want to live out what they saw as an
intolerably slow dying, painful, undignified and expensive. These
signposts pointed me towards the dread with which some approach
their last days and towards the schemes and secrets they hold as
they look for a better passage. They also prompted my thinking
about how we help people end their lives with dignity, and how we
fail. In both of these cases, the person was older and seriously
ailing. Although neither had a diagnosed terminal illness, each
chose to end his life in anticipation of a long dying process, and
each chose suicide not only to relieve his own fears and agony, but
to spare his family from the burdens of his care.

Matt

Matt was approaching his eightieth birthday when he got up before dawn on the morning he died. He eased himself quietly out of the bed he had shared with his wife of almost fifty years and headed down to the kitchen of their old farmhouse in the mountains of East Tennessee. He took a last sip of the bourbon that kept his hands steady, wrote a brief note, and went outdoors into the first beams of sunlight under the apple tree. Raising his gun, he shot himself cleanly in the temple and fell there, dead.

His wife heard the shot, and, fearing something awful, ran downstairs and outside, where she found him. She called her son-in-law who lived close by.

"You better come over. I think Daddy got shot because he has a hole in his head," she told him.

Matt's was not an impulsive act. His health had been worsening over the years from the toll of heavy drinking, diabetes, painful ear infections, and then Parkinson's. His family were full of suggestions about what he should do, what he should eat, how he should fight these health issues, but Matt had never been a slave to other people's opinions, no matter how well meant. He still worked on his farm daily, but his strength was failing, and he didn't like what he saw coming. He'd had a little preview of this during a recent visit to his brother Joe, in a nearby nursing home. Joe had both emphysema and advanced diabetes and had undergone several amputations—some toes, then his lower leg, then a hand. His care was costing tens of thousands of dollars a year, resources Joe hated to see dwindling as he worried about his wife's well being. And Joe was now wearing diapers, an indignity Matt found repugnant.

It seemed odd, but after that visit, Matt actually seemed more upbeat. He reached out to friends, spent time daily with his nearby daughter. Some good times lay ahead. He and his wife were preparing to celebrate their fiftieth anniversary and his eightieth birthday, and the baptism of his first grandson and namesake was coming in the next two months—so many milestones to savor, so much family would be swirling around him, the beloved patriarch. Why couldn't he wait? What made him act when he did?

I found out about Matt's suicide just a day later when his cousin who attended my church called to let me know. She was confused and grieving about this sudden loss and wanted to talk. Through her I realized how many questions surrounded this shocking act and how hard it was for her and Matt's immediate family to make any sense of it.

As it happened, just a few weeks later, I had plans to do a wedding in Knoxville, not too far from where Matt and his family lived. I was hoping to be able to meet and talk with them, even though my connection through the cousin wasn't that close.

Graciously, the widow and Matt's grown daughter and son who lived nearby agreed to talk with me. Sitting around their kitchen table in the farmhouse, in surprisingly open conversations, I learned some of the specifics described above and began to realize how very complicated were the reactions of the people around Matt.

First was shock—no one had seen this coming, and this was a violent death, no matter how expert the shot. Their husband, father, and grandfather was so suddenly, unexpectedly gone. There was anger as well. Matt had always been very independent, wanted to do things his own way, but how could he do this? And how could his timing be so off, so seemingly cruel? What about the anniversary, the birthday, the baptism—weren't they things to look forward to, reasons to hold off? If he'd as least waited a few months, wouldn't this have been less painful?

Surprisingly, even as these family members told me of their initial raw feelings, they were already beginning to change their grasp on what had happened. The daughter, particularly, was able to see that "what Daddy did was out of love, especially for our mother." He didn't want her to have to go through what his brother's wife did, didn't want her to have to be there for the long slow decline, the hemorrhage of money, the gradual lessening of all of his powers as he became an invalid. He actually thought that what he did was better for all of them, children and grandchildren as well. He was willing to miss some of what might have been remaining good time for him so that he could die on his own terms and spare them all having to watch him suffer. These, at least, were the conjectures of his daughter.

Matt's wife had come to a similar place of acceptance and understanding. She was no longer angry, just sad and wanting to protect Matt's good reputation in the community. Their son had taken over the running of the farm far sooner than he ever expected; he was stoic, loyal, hard to read.

This was the first time I had been close to the suicide of an older person who simply wanted to avoid what he saw ahead for himself and who wanted to spare his family the burdens of seeing him through it. At first there was shock, then anger and pain, then love emerged, strangely, from this unexpected, violent act. I was grateful for the opportunity they gave me to enter into their story and hear even the trivial details: Matt's wife saw that his bourbon glass still had beads of moisture on it as it sat on the table, obviously not long before the planned shot. She did something with the gun; none of the others knew what. Apparently there was no legal investigation of this obvious suicide. An old farmer, perhaps despairing as he looked ahead, perhaps confident he was making a good choice, or perhaps, as a son-in-law suggested, just "sick and tired of being sick and tired," had ended his life, at the moment and in the manner of his own choosing.

Larry

Another signpost for me was the suicide of Larry, the father of a friend. He jumped off his apartment building to his death when he was eighty-two, laying his glasses and watch neatly on the flat roof from which he leapt, sailing by his own window where his wife briefly noted a passing shadow.

Several months before, Larry had fallen and had a small stroke, some brain injury and hospitalization. Larry's prognosis was poor, and his life had become unhappy. The wife he'd left his first family for so many years earlier had turned into a grasping shrew, and he couldn't lose himself on the country club golf course anymore; he saw nothing to live for except diminishment. And so, in the hospital just after the stroke, he hoarded pills and got hold of a plastic bag and used his pillow to try to die. Caught in the act, he was sent off to the psychiatrist to be convinced that his life was worth living. Once Larry convinced the shrink that he'd been convinced, he hatched Plan B. He had a long, fond lunch with one of his sons, asked that they drive out to the old Foxborough Hunt Club where he'd been such a fine golfer, such a *bon vivant*. He was wistful as he gazed around him, remembering the days that would never be again. Once back at his apartment, he declined his son's offer to go up to the apartment, said it was such a beautiful day, he wanted to stroll around a bit. And up he went to the roof.

His family hushed this up as if it was shameful, and the obituary gave no cause of death. One of his sons was very angry; his daughter was devastated. Another son called me for consolation, knowing I was a priest. He choked up as he talked. Although not particularly religious, he wanted to know if what his father had done was a sin.

"Do you think my father will go to hell?" he asked.

I tried to reassure him. No, it was not a sin, and no, I didn't believe he would go to hell; I didn't even believe in that kind of hell. The family tried to make sense, tried to see it as a reach for freedom and not a rejection, not a disgrace. His sons and daughter remembered the beautiful letter he had written to them all five years before—how long had he been plotting this? To me it seemed such a sad, desperate move, made in the absence of compassionate support that could perhaps have brightened Larry's last days, or if not that, at least helped him to end them non-violently.

A "Mercy Killing" in South Carolina

In January of 2018, an article by Zach Fox appeared in the online newsletter, *Goupstate.com*, about a man shooting his parents to death the previous November. Fox gives a poignant account of the desperation of a couple who no longer wanted to go on living due to extreme illness and debilitation, and the dilemma that was posed in those circumstances for their son who cared for them. The mother had suffered from strokes and had lost the ability to walk or care for herself and could barely communicate. The father had begun drinking heavily, and had become angry and violently abusive. He often talked of suicide and several times asked his son to shoot him and his wife.

"I could not count the times he asked me to shoot him and momma," David Belcher said. "I knew he was serious." Finally, even his mother joined the plea, saying, "Son, do what your dad asked." The son pled guilty to voluntary manslaughter to avoid a murder conviction and was sentenced to ten years in prison despite his own and his siblings' conviction that what he did was out of love, and a mercy, and at the request of his parents.

This is a tragic story, and there is so much about it that could have been different, had our laws and our cultural attitude towards end-of-life situations been different. First of all, one wonders about whether the mother, aged sixty-nine, could have had better care, whether in-home or in a hospice, and what prevented her from receiving this. Did the family lack the means to pay for such care, or did she insist on being at home with only her son to care for her and her husband? And surely the husband, also only sixty-nine, could have gone on living and gotten help in addressing his addiction, rage, and probably depression, whether or not his wife was still alive.

But let's assume both parents considered their lives intolerable and no longer wanted to live. Did they have a right to request such "mercy" from their son, or should they have managed to end their lives themselves? What if the mother had written out explicit advance directives asking for aid in dying should she ever reach an extreme state of disability? Even if aid in dying was illegal in South Carolina, which it is, perhaps her directives could have included a desire to stop receiving food and liquids, or VSED (Voluntary Stopping of Eating and Drinking; more on this directive below). If the family, parents and all three children, had talked about this directive and agreed to help their mother when the time came, perhaps she could have died in a non-violent way, but still in accordance with her clearly stated wishes. And perhaps, if the husband had been able to support his wife in honoring her directives, he might have gotten his own life back on track and had a fairly good quality of life for some years.

It is saddening as well to consider the situation of the son, the one sibling apparently able to care for the parents, and the stress of this responsibility. Can we imagine that he snapped one day, exhausted, overwhelmed, hating to see the misery of his parents? With repeated requests from his father to kill them, and then his mother's assent, can we see him picking up the gun as a last resort, a tortured, unnatural act of love? And then why did he go, covering the bodies with sheets, leaving them to be found ten days later? Was he in shock, frozen with remorse or fear by what he had done?

I am certain this story is not unique, that others like it happen more frequently than we know. I ache so much for these families. Their last illnesses and deaths could be so much more humane and dignified if we allowed relief through well-crafted aid-in-dying laws.

Tyler: A Dog's Death

It may seem odd to include the euthanasia of a dog in this section, but I do so because of the contrast Tyler's story makes with the deaths of Matt and Larry and the couple in South Carolina. My son, Chris, adopted Tyler when he was in college. An adorable little brown and white puppy with a freckled nose, Tyler was a hunting dog, a fraternity house dog, an affectionate, fairly well behaved pet. When Chris left for San Francisco several years later to become a chef, Tyler came to live with me, first on the banks of the Potomac River in Maryland where he could run free, and later in my house in Chevy Chase where his runs and walks were always on leashes.

I loved him as much as Chris did. Tyler was my loyal companion during four years of living alone, and then, when Chris and his wife and tiny daughter came to live with me for two years, Tyler was a beloved member of the household. He was slowing down by then at almost thirteen years of age, and no longer wanting long walks, happy instead to lie around the house and sneak up onto the couch whenever possible. Some months after Chris returned, Tyler began showing signs of illness, some lumps, occasional incontinence and general fatigue. The vet said he had lymphoma and there wasn't really much that could be done except to keep him comfortable. That fall, as Thanksgiving neared, we realized Tyler was dying a slow death, with more and more discomfort and less and less zest for anything, not for food, or walks, or us. We had hoped Tyler would make it to Thanksgiving, but by the Monday before, he seemed so down and aching that we called the vet and asked if we might bring him by for a check. Neither Chris nor I had the heart to initiate a conversation about putting him down. But once at the animal hospital, after a quick assessment the vet said, "If it were my dog, I'd put him down now." And so we did, Chris and I standing on either side of Tyler, holding and patting him as the doctor inserted a needle in one leg. Tyler gave a brief flinch and then was still. After a few moments we thanked the vet and walked to the car, both crying, but knowing we'd done the right thing.

Tyler had lived a long, full life; he had been spared more suffering; and his death had been quick and painless, a peaceful end, a compassionate good-bye. I can't help but contrast the mercy of euthanasia for pets with the agony faced by so many humans living through the final stages of disease and impairment that they would choose to avoid if they could.

These deaths—two suicides, a "mercy killing" and one animal euthanasia—informed my consciousness and stayed with me as I worked as a pastor and became more and more attuned to the dilemmas encountered by people as they faced their deaths.

Books, Articles, Films

The list of books, films and articles about aid in dying is long, and in most of them, a case can be made for at least the morality of such assistance, if not, sadly, in most cases, the legality. While I refer to

other books and articles throughout this argument, I will di
three well-known books and films on this subject here.

Anne Lamott, in a chapter from her book, *Grace (Eventually)*,
entitled "At Death's Window," tells of helping a friend die, after
the friend and his wife had asked her for this help, by feeding him
a lethal dose of barbiturates that she had obtained "through wily
underground ways" (96). They had discussed it several times and
were very clear in their desires. Anne herself was a committed
Christian who had this to say, rather blithely: " I believe that life is
a kind of Earth School, so even though assisted suicide means
you're getting out early, before the term ends, you're going to be
leaving anyway, so who says it isn't okay to take an incomplete in
the course?" (94).

I would disagree that this kind of death is an "incomplete," and
would see it instead as a compassionate, loving completion of a
life—an end that is peaceful, dignified and in accordance with the
dying person's sense of his own narrative and degree of control over
it. I have no idea how any legal issues were dealt with by Lamott
and her friend's wife, and as her book is in the public domain, I
suspect no problems ensued.

In another book, Anna Quindlen's best-selling novel, *One
True Thing*, written in 1994 and later made into a movie starring
Meryl Streep in an Oscar-nominated performance, the assisted

death of an older mother and wife suffering from terminal cancer is the subject of a criminal investigation. In that case, the act of feeding the barbiturates was clearly illegal and the perpetrator faced serious penalties. The suspense and questions raised make for not only a real page-turner, but also a moral inventory of what is at stake in these kinds of deaths.

More recently, the bestselling novel by Lisa Genova, *Still Alice* (later made into a movie with Julianne Moore in the Oscar-winning title role), tells the story of a woman diagnosed with early-onset Alzheimer's. The impact, from its earliest signs, on her, her family, and on her career as a college professor is clearly shown. Her embarrassment as she tries to hide her increasingly obvious affliction is painful to witness. Eventually, she tries to execute her carefully planned computer plot. She has instructed herself to open a certain file once a set of questions no longer make sense to her. The file contains specific instructions about taking lethal medications she has hidden away in her bureau drawer. She thought she'd figured this all out back before her mind no longer worked. But the plan fails; she can't follow the instructions, she drops the pills all over the floor just as a daughter walks in on her and puts an end to any further possibility of suicide. The dreaded decline of Alice's mental state continues, and although the book and movie seem to want to tell us that she is still capable of love and that is all that matters, we are left with the huge questions about what is enough to make life still meaningful and worth living, and who is to be the judge of that.

Carol

I now turn to the situations of real people who have dementia, and how their stories differ from situations where people are of sound mind, and whether aid in dying may or may not have been an option. My first up-close connection with a dementia patient was daunting, frustrating, occasionally amusing, and educational.

In 1997, I had a seven-month interim position on the staff of Grace Cathedral in San Francisco. My main responsibility was to develop an adult education program, but I shared pastoral work with the rest of the clergy staff. Perhaps because I was the new girl in town, I was asked to go and visit Carol, who had Alzheimer's.

I went to her home in a nice section of the city, one of those large, pastel-colored Victorian houses perched on a hillside. And there was little Carol, timidly opening the door, all dressed to go out in a warm coat, scarf and gloves. It was early April, a lovely warm spring day, about seventy degrees. I told her who I was and got a blank look, but when I mentioned that I was from the church where she used to bake the cakes for coffee hours and receptions, her face flickered with a tiny smile of recognition, and she ushered me in. I said I had come to bring communion, and there was no need to keep her coat on while we visited. We sat on her couch. I tried to think of something to say, and, hearing noises upstairs, asked if she was having some work done on the house.

"Oh, no, that's my husband," she said.

At that point a caregiver tiptoed in, saying, "Carol has a plumber at work upstairs."

Not wanting to contradict or further confuse Carol, I moved on, saying I wanted to arrange my little communion set right there in front of the couch. As I took out the small paten and chalice, the dollhouse-sized linens, the tiny flagon of wine and container of communion wafers, Carol was clearly baffled. She reached to play with them as though they really were dollhouse toys, and soon I realized how silly this was, and what an odd thing to do with this poor floundering woman! Why bring miniature tokens of something she probably wouldn't recognize even if it were the real thing in church? Why present something that may once have been meaningful as if it were a child's game? Was I making a travesty of the sacrament?

Dismayed, I looked across the room at the grand piano in the corner. Hoping to make a meaningful connection, I said, somewhat desperately, "Oh, Carol, what a lovely piano. Do you play, or did you?"

Carol's eyes brightened. "Would you like to play?" she asked.

I moved to the piano, and Carol followed eagerly. As it happened, I did know one piece by heart—a very easy *Gymnopedie* by Erik Satie, and I started in, slowly, tentatively. But Carol responded immediately.

"I know that piece!" she said, swaying in time with its quiet chords.

I was delighted! We did have a connection here: Carol was engaged with this music, so much so that soon she settled herself right next to me on the piano bench. We were cozy, happy, on even footing, whereas before we had been estranged and separated by the fog and confusion of her disease. Each of the several times I visited Carol after that, I went to her piano, rummaged around in piles of music to find things I could play and settled in with her for some real companionship. Her illness had not yet robbed her of this response to music, and it was the music, far more than the sacrament I had brought, that gave meaning to our time. In music, we found true communion.

Until then I had not known that this ability to remember and respond to music long after other cognitive functions have severely diminished was a feature of Alzheimer's. This realization was to prove valuable several years later with my own father and other Alzheimer's patients I have visited since. Always, music, whether part of a nursing home chapel service or played by me on the piano, would seem to get through to the person, to connect with some not-yet-destroyed memories. As Carol had done, people would move in time to the rhythm, or even sing the words, sometimes all the words, even if they could otherwise barely utter a single sentence! I realized that, in thinking about advanced dementia and what comprises meaningful life and relationship, music could be a lingering gift that can still connect us, still bring its delights from an earlier life to the awkward and frustrating visits where normal conversation is no longer possible.

I first learned this from Carol, and I thank her for it. Music helped me befriend her, and several years later, it became the one fragile, remaining link to my father.

TWO

The Moral and Spiritual Abyss of Dementia

Before further considering stories about end-of-life decisions that involve the deliberate taking of life, or help in doing so for someone who desires this, it is important that we establish clear definitions about such choices and their moral implications. For instance, when I tentatively mentioned that I was doing some writing about helping people with advanced dementia die, my mother replied immediately, "I'm against suicide." And when my sister suggested that Dad's insulin for diabetes should be withdrawn during his last months of Alzheimer's, the nurse on his locked ward responded tartly, "That would be murder!" It will be important as we consider moral and legal questions that the various terms now in use about aid in dying are well defined and not confused with each other.

Definitions

"Suicide": 1. The act or instance of taking one's own life voluntarily and intentionally, esp. by a person of years of discretion and of sound mind (*Merriam-Webster Ninth New Collegiate Dictionary*).

"Assisted Suicide": Suicide committed by someone with assistance from another person," and

"Physician-assisted Suicide (PAS)": suicide by a patient facilitated by means (such as a drug prescription) or by information (such as indication of a lethal dosage) provided by a physician aware of the patient's intent (*Merriam-Webster.com*).

"Aid in Dying": A preferred term in current usage. This is the same as assisted suicide or PAS, but avoids the negative and violent connotations of the word, "suicide," and conveys that these deaths are in response to clearly stated requests by a person already anticipating or actually in the process of dying.

"Euthanasia": The act of killing an individual for reasons considered merciful (from the Greek, *eu*, meaning "good," and *thanatos*, meaning "death") (*The American Heritage Dictionary*).

Euthanasia can be confused with PAS, but differs because a person other than a physician might administer the lethal dose, usually because the dying person, particularly one who is severely demented, is incapable of self-administration. Euthanasia may or may not be administered in response to a stated or written request.

Other terms: "Assisted dying" is sometimes used as an umbrella term for "assisted suicide" and "euthanasia." It is an example of a trend by advocates to replace the word "suicide" with "dying," "death" or ideally, "aid in dying," as described above, perhaps because of the stigma and shame that still surround some suicides and assisted deaths. Also in common use are: "physician-assisted dying," "physician-assisted death," "death with dignity," "right to die," "compassionate death," "compassionate dying," "end-of-life choice," and "medical assistance at the end of life."

Moral and Spiritual Concerns

One reason consideration of aid in dying is so fraught, even for people of sound mind, is that it does indeed involve either suicide or euthanasia. Taking a life always entails serious moral concerns. The major religious groups—Abrahamic (Judaism, Christianity, Islam), Dharmic (Hinduism, Buddhism, Jainism, Sikh) and Neo-

Pagan (Wicca)—all condemn suicide to varying degrees and under varying circumstances. The main reason for this condemnation in most of these traditions is a belief in the sanctity of life, and in many cases, in non-violence. Suicide is seen as a form of murder—self-murder—and is thus condemned as such in the Judeo-Christian tradition, rooted in the Mosaic commandment to do no murder. Suicide can be seen as an act of ultimate despair, denying the gift and meaning of life, even denying God. When this happens in the case of a depressed person, especially a young person, it is almost always seen as tragic, something to be prevented.

Some traditions do allow for suicide as a way of avoiding suffering at the end of life. Sherwin Nuland, in his influential book, *How We Die: Reflections on Life's Final Chapter*, points out a couple of exceptions to the standard general opposition to suicide. For Nuland, these are "the unendurable infirmities of a crippling old age and the final devastations of terminal disease." He continues: "The nouns are not important in that last sentence—it is the adjectives that cry out for attention, for they are the very crux of the issue and will tolerate no compromise or 'well, almost's: *unendurable, crippling, final* and *terminal*" (151). Nuland then takes us back to the words of the great orator of the first century, Seneca the Elder, and his thoughts on old age:

I will not relinquish old age if it leaves my better part intact. But if it begins to take my mind, if it destroys its faculties one by one, if it leave me not life but breath, I will depart from the putrid or tottering edifice. I will not escape by death from disease so long as it may be healed, and leaves my mind unimpaired. I will not raise my hand against myself on account of pain, for so to die is to be conquered. But I know that if I must suffer without hope of relief, I will depart, not through fear of the pain itself, but because it prevents all for which I would live. (151)

Some other forms of suicide have been deemed acceptable in some cultures. Suicide as a way of preserving one's honor, as in the Japanese ritual suicide known as hara-kiri, is one. In our own and other cultures, dueling as a way of defending one's honor was acceptable for centuries, a custom in which usually one person died after voluntarily putting himself at risk. Almost a suicide, even though at the hand of another, a duel brought to a tragic end the life of one of our foremost American founders, Alexander Hamilton. On the other hand, suicides undertaken as a form of terrorism, for example, by suicide bombers or the 9/11 killers, as a way of destroying others while achieving martyrdom, are clearly unacceptable in orthodox Islamic teaching. Classic Roman Catholic orthodoxy considers suicide a sin, again, because it seems a denial of the sanctity of life. A related argument is that suicide or aid in dying is "playing God." Never mind that with modern medicine we regularly intervene to save lives that would otherwise end—why is it only "playing God" when we intervene to end a long, agonizing, painful death?

But if we set aside strict adherence to orthodoxy, as our society increasingly does, then moral questions surrounding suicide and aid in dying become more nuanced and difficult. Context and motive become highly relevant as we think about the circumstances of those who might choose to end their lives and might need help in doing so.

Another argument advanced by those against suicide or aid in dying in the face of terminal illness is a belief that suffering is somehow noble, even an inspiration to others. "She was so strong," they say, after watching a long tortured dying. "He fought it to the end," they say after a poor exhausted soul finally dies in the ICU after all possible desperate measures have been tried. There is indeed some virtue in suffering bravely borne during many of life's difficult passages, but when life is at an end, and recovery is not possible, then it would seem that a patient's interest in alleviating his suffering should be honored above abstract ideals held by others about what that suffering might represent. The "nobility" of fighting hard against a disease also implies that a person who chooses not to fight the inevitable is, somehow, weak or less admirable, and I call that nonsense! It takes at least as much courage to accept the inevitable as it does to fight it.

Among the many conversations that urge compassion in considering ways of helping people end their lives, or at least shorten their dying process to reduce suffering, are those of Atul Gawande, a physician and acclaimed writer. His best-selling book, *Being Mortal*, published in 2014, thoughtfully encourages people to discuss with family members, doctors, and perhaps clergy what their wishes are for the ends of their lives. He recommends that they do this well before death stares them in the face. He traces how woefully rare and incomplete these conversations have been, leading to the sad result of too many people dying in ICU's, too many people floundering when confronted by heroic medical attempts to defeat death at all costs—by definition an impossible quest. Gawande offers a wide array of case histories and examples of how people, when given the chance, will opt for quality of life over length of life. He stresses how much the values people hold should be honored and included in their thinking about end-of-life care, which is so much what I wish we had been able to do with my father. Gawande traces the development of the nursing home industry even as he points out how much being in one's own home is preferred to such facilities, and he recognizes that personal autonomy is something most of us want even to the ends of our lives as much as possible. To this end, he writes at length about the value of palliative care—given not to cure illness but to provide relief from the symptoms and stress of a serious illness. The goal is to improve quality of life for both the patient and the family.

Gawande touches only very briefly on assisted suicide as an option for those facing intractable pain and suffering, and he worries that its availability, such as in the Netherlands, might actually work against efforts to provide better and more universally available palliative care. His worry seems to be that it might seem a more efficient alternative, robbing people of the benefits of palliative care, and this seems to me a reasonable argument.

Gawande's important work and that of so many others now supporting palliative and hospice care for the dying are gaining widespread support, not only among patients but also in the medical community. Doctors, who have traditionally been focused completely on defeating or at least delaying death, are becoming more open to quality-of-life concerns, especially in the face of terminal illness. All of this is good news.

The bad news is how little consideration is given to the particular case of those with advanced dementia. Today about five million people in the United States have Alzheimer's, where it is the sixth leading cause of death. As *The Sydney (Australia) Morning Herald* reported on February 7, 2017, "decades of research have not produced a single drug that alters its course." Given the rising number of aging people in our population, five million could become two or three times that number by 2050, and the goals of the increasing millions of dollars spent on research are as much in search of ways to slow the progress or delay the onset of this dread disease as on finding a so-far elusive cure.

Palliative care may serve well for those who have some use of their cognitive faculties; it can make a real difference in handling physical pain, disability and suffering. In these cases, patients are no longer kept alive or put on life support if death is near and there is no hope of cure. Chemotherapy and other intrusive and in themselves painful therapies are discontinued. Morphine is dispensed liberally enough to control intractable pain, even if doing so hastens death by depressing respiration. Hospice care is widely available and increasingly chosen when people enter the dying process. After weighing quality of life over length of life, more and more people are having serious and important conversations with their family and caregivers about their deaths. They want "a good death"; they want to die at home; they want to be with the people they love; they don't want to be in pain; and they want to retain some measure of physical dignity and control.

In fact, autonomy is becoming a major criterion for evaluating options at the end of life and a major argument for aid in dying. As the philosopher, Ronald Dworkin, wrote in his 1986 essay, "On Autonomy and the Demented Self":

> "The value of autonomy...lies in the scheme of responsibility it creates: autonomy makes each of us responsible for shaping his own life according to some coherent and instinctive sense of character, conviction and interest. It allows us to lead our own lives rather than be led along them, so that each of us can be, to the extent such a scheme of rights can make this possible, what he has made himself." (Quoted in *Being Mortal*, 140)

But for patients to take this responsibility, society demands that they be of sound mind. Advance directives, as currently written, usually cover only withdrawal or withholding of treatment when death is near. Ideally, the dying person has stated his intentions orally and in writing to his family and medical team so that they can co-operate in fulfilling them. And, for this population, if they live in states where aid in dying is now a legal option, autonomy can be extended to include this. But how can autonomy be honored for those whose mental capacities have been ravaged by late-stage dementia? How can self-rule, or autonomy, be honored if there is no self? It is a tragic oxymoron. There seems to be a collective denial about how dementia patients are truly left out of discussions about aid in dying. For those in advanced stages, even palliative care becomes little more than feeding, cleaning and the maintenance of a body whose selfhood has all but vanished.

In addition to whatever denial exists in talking about the end of life, an extra moral burden seems attached to the idea of aid in dying for dementia patients who are incompetent to ask for or cooperate in such a death just when their earlier self would have begged for it. When a person has died in mind but not in body, that person can't hasten death, either on her own or even with help. She has no way of freeing herself from the entire course of dementia through to its extreme late-stage unless some other malady rescues her.

This area is fraught with legal and moral implications. Unlike the administration of morphine or fentanyl that has become increasingly acceptable in easing the dying process at the end of life for mentally competent patients, any kind of hastening of death in an Alzheimer's patient could be seen at best as without clear consent, and is more likely to be seen as euthanasia, which remains a legal taboo everywhere in this country. Unlike for those of sound mind, suicide seems unlikely for someone with advanced Alzheimer's; as in the cases discussed above in the first chapter, "Signposts," some people who decide life is no longer worth living are capable of carefully planning their suicides. I'm not talking here of depression, clinical or otherwise, but of terminal illness that will lead to extreme pain, disfigurement and/or loss of all dignity. These deaths happen more than most people realize, and they are possible because the people who choose them have the mental capacity to will and carry out a suicide.

The concept of "brain death" in cases of coma or persistent vegetative state led to the legally accepted withdrawing of life support, allowing people to die even if their hearts were still beating, and this was a compassionate new way of thinking about death. As more and more people reach older ages, and therefore Alzheimer's and other forms of dementia become more common, I hope we can overcome the present stigma of aid in dying for people thus afflicted. Aid in dying is not an alternative to doing everything possible toward finding a cure or slowing the progress of the disease, but it is an option we must not ignore. We are dealing with diseases of the brain, and we need to start now to talk about them and figure out how to deal with people whose personhood gradually dies due to impaired brain function even though the body lives on.

I am wondering about advance directives that would cover situations in which a person could specify the circumstances in which he would want to shorten his life. Further, the person could even spell out the means he would choose, with the clear intention that, should those circumstances of extreme dementia arise, he would have what support he needed to shorten his life in the way he had willed when he was of sound mind. For example, someone might say that if she could no longer recognize anyone and could no longer speak or interact with others, she would not wish to continue living. Added conditions might include all the indignities of incontinence and not being able to feed one's self, although those alone would not be sufficient cause. (For me, humiliation or indignity, no matter how unpleasant, is not sufficient cause to shorten my life. I do think there is a benefit in going through such things with as much grace as one can muster—and this goes for caregivers as well. Life throws a lot of stuff at us that we don't want or think we can't handle, and the ability to endure hardship may be a character-building strength to be cultivated and admired—when the sufferer is aware of his situation.)

So, although factors of humiliation and even financial concerns might be taken into consideration as aggravating conditions, the decisive factors would be the loss of power to communicate in any meaningful way and little or no recognition of anyone. The writing of extremely specific directives would be absolutely crucial, as well as the discussion of the same with caregivers before dementia advances too far. I do think there would need to be room for subjectivity and individual choice here, and that medical standards of exactly what constitutes life or death are only part of the picture.

What is really at issue is "a life worth living." One person might not agree with another on just what constitutes "a life worth living," but a person facing dementia may be very sure that when she no longer has a recognizable self, she does not want her body to go on living.

I was for a while in a retirement group where people discussed circumstances that, for them, would render life no longer worth living. In the case of dementia, there was general agreement about what folks believed would be intolerable for them. Most seemed to feel that there should be a way for severely demented patients to be helped if it was clear, due to good directives, that they had reached a state in which they would not longer want to go on living. Interestingly enough, the biggest concern seemed to be how to protect loved ones from legal liability if a demented person's life was shortened with any kind of cooperation from these caregivers.

Certainly any such directives would have to be carefully discussed with family members well before the dementia had robbed the person of judgment and mental clarity. Because aid in dying is illegal in most states, there would need to be some way to protect folks who would be in a position to offer support. It is likely that such scenarios could play out in a private home; they would be much more difficult in a nursing home or even hospice situation. For example, had my father been at home, shortening his life through insulin withdrawal might have been a legal possibility, had we had clear directives and a consensus among his wife and children that that is what he would have wanted. A distinction is rightly drawn between withdrawing something life-sustaining and actually doing something to end life, even if the result is the same. However, even with directives and consensus, there would have been legal liability issues.

Mental competence, or "decisional capacity" (helpful words from a column by George Will in *The Washington Post*, Aug. 28, 2015) is one criterion in each state that allows for aid in dying; once a person no longer has decisional capacity, assisted suicide becomes a moral quagmire. I should note here, that with mentally incompetent persons, the line between aid in dying and euthanasia becomes extremely blurry as the patient might be beyond the point at which he could ingest the lethal medicine himself. Such a death would really be euthanasia with previous permission. I would see such assisted deaths as actually honoring the value of human life by mercifully ending it when all that makes it human has been stolen away into the abyss of late-stage dementia. Here all the questions of what a patient would choose now, or would have chosen before, become almost impossible to answer, either by the patient or anyone else, if the patient hadn't previously made them known.

Assisted death in the face of advanced dementia can be seen as an affirmation of the goodness of life and the fullness of personhood once sickness has robbed someone of those very things. Assisted death with advanced dementia announces that, at certain times, a human being's life is so debased, so lacking in the ability to communicate, so devoid of dignity and any semblance of the person who once was, that this life is barely human at all except in a physiological sense. When this happens, aid in dying can re-affirm the autonomy of a person in the face of a long and agonizing death. It can be an act of acceptance and compassion for what a person is up against. It can express love for all those whose lives could be overwhelmed by the long ordeal of caring for someone who is no longer truly there. It can have huge economic effects, not just on families, but on society as a whole and the priorities we place on various kinds of medical care.

Given the hefty moral valence of end-of-life choices in the case of dementia patients, it is no surprise that both family and professional caregivers may weigh the questions differently and come to different conclusions, depending on what each feels to be most at stake, what values are being honored or betrayed. Given this circumstance, what seems most important is that people have options and that patients and family members, along with doctors and perhaps clergy, speak very honestly with each other. Rather than passively assenting to the onset of dementia, patients and families should have conversations beginning with the question, "How do you want your life to end?" I now wish that my family had done this when my father began to lose his mind.

THREE

The Story of Dad

I walk slowly down the corridor of the Alzheimer's wing, holding Dad's hand, stopping occasionally to comment on small things he would notice—a bit of trash on the rug, an open door. "What's out there?" he asks. As I walk, I realize that he had done this very same thing with me, some sixty years ago! My father had walked with me when I was a little toddler in diapers, tenderly holding my hand and answering my endless questions patiently, doing it out of love. So perhaps it was fitting that now, towards the end of his life, I would do for him what he did so willingly for me at the beginning of my life. I am comforted in that moment, feeling that there is a rightness in our slow, gentle walk. At that point, I feel that he is still Dad, still aware of being with me even if not sure exactly who I was.

Some months later, I sat at Dad's bedside in a recovery facility where he had been moved while he healed from a broken leg. He would never walk on his own again. He didn't seem to know who I was. He didn't talk. His blanket had been brushed aside; his diapers were clearly visible. I didn't know what to do. Finally, I began lightly stroking his legs below the knee, just as I had when my siblings and I were small and he paid us each a nickel for a leg rub as he lay on the couch on a Saturday afternoon, dozing, or trying to. I felt nostalgia for those sweet childhood efforts and wondered if he remembered, as I ran my fingers over his calves, who I was or that I used to do this a long time ago. I could discern no reaction.

And then, after that and every other visit, I would go to my car and cry, cry hard and long and wrenchingly about the father I'd lost, the father who had died, probably two or three years earlier, really, but continuing on in a "life" he would abhor. Along with grief, I felt helplessness, frustration and usually, finally, anger. This was not what Dad would have wanted. What a cruel irony that his life would end in this way, that he would be demented, crippled, incontinent and institutionalized—a man of huge intelligence, an athlete who thrived on exercise, a man of dignity and reserve, and a man who relished independence and free choice! A man who had told me all those years ago that if things ever came to this, he wouldn't want to be alive.

Robert Mann was born on January 7, 1918 in Pittsburgh, Pennsylvania to an engineer and a schoolteacher, both hard-working Presbyterians of Scotch-Irish descent. His parents had married late in life for the time; each was thirty-two, and Robert was the second of their two children, the younger brother of Jane. She was a rebel, a beautiful, willful girl, and perhaps in reaction, "Roddy" was a straight arrow, a top student, an obedient and respectful son. He went to Cornell University on scholarship, sent his laundry home weekly, washed dishes in his fraternity house for extra cash, and only cautiously began to savor beer and parties and the company of girls. His parents were teetotalers, so he grew up feeling that alcohol was a sin—as was tobacco, although his father smoked. Like many young people then, he was "saving himself for marriage," which he expected to be traditional—he the breadwinner, his wife a stay-at-home mother and loyal helpmeet.

Despite these prudent ways, young Robert had a devilish and playful side, especially when he was with his best friend, Knox Harper. Halloween was their favorite holiday, and tricks were real tricks—throwing eggs and rotten tomatoes with zest, squirting shaving cream with abandon and running neighborhood dogs to the edge of town, all great sport, though naughty. And dropping a glass bottle of milk and then catching it on the way down was huge, although risky, fun.

For Robert and Knox, humor about people who were insane was their specialty. Only a few miles from Ben Avon, their suburb of Pittsburgh, was Dixmont, a state hospital for the mentally ill. It was a huge place, with forbidding gray walls standing on a high bluff overlooking the highway and the Ohio River. Driving by, they would imagine the horrors within, padded cells, men in white coats restraining the patients, a cacophony of wild, mindless cries echoing through this "loony bin." Robert and Knox even wrote poems, doggerel, really, about Dixmont, or the "nuthouse" and the "fiends" within. I suppose this wasn't considered to be the sick, uncaring humor then that it would be today, but it certainly must have shaped my father's feelings about mental illness or losing one's mind. In hindsight, I can imagine that this childhood joking about the insane presaged his later horror at the prospect of dementia, something to be deeply feared, avoided at all costs.

After Cornell, Bob Mann moved to Philadelphia where he took a job at an engineering firm. He soon met Betty Swartley at the Presbyterian Church in Germantown where she lived. She was a recent graduate of Hood College and, like most women in 1941, was interested in finding a husband, preferably a tall one, and settling down. Bob was indeed tall, and handsome. After about a year of courtship, he asked her to marry him during an outing to Hershey, Pennsylvania. Newly engaged, they heard about the

Japanese attack on Pearl Harbor on that fateful December Sunday, but Bob was spared military service because his work was considered crucial to the war effort. They married in March of 1942, had a lavish reception hosted by Betty's wealthy uncle at a local country club, and headed off on their honeymoon. As my mother later described it, they were two scared virgins on a road trip to Florida, and barely said a word as they drove to Wilmington, Delaware for their wedding night.

After a brief stint in New York City, where I was born, Bob and Betty moved back to suburban Philadelphia, where they had three more children in well-planned succession, each of us two-and-a-half years apart. My father worked his way up in the engineering firm, but finally realized he needed to make a change due to limited prospects there. After a disastrous year in Bethlehem, Pennsylvania at a firm that went bankrupt, his life took a dramatic turn. His own father, Harvey Mann, ran a small family company, Mann Engineering, with a younger partner who suddenly died of a heart attack. Harvey needed help, and Dad needed a job, so he began commuting to Pittsburgh during the week. Then, just a few months later, Dad's mother died of cancer, and just a month after that, his father died too, of a sudden heart attack. Dad now owned half of Mann Engineering, and he moved his family in 1956 to Sewickley, a vaunted suburban enclave of old money from steel and other heavy industry.

Bob successfully grew his company and prospered into a level of affluence he had probably never anticipated. Our family lived in a big house; we children went to private schools and then on to elite colleges. Vacation travel grew ever more upscale as Dad savored both his love of gathering the whole family together on trips for shared adventure and his passion for seeing as much of the world as possible. He was proud that he'd travelled to all continents except Antarctica, and he loved the pleasure my mother took in luxury cruises and fine hotels.

Much of this material success was based on Dad's intelligence, determination, and will power. He was definitely a believer in hard work and achievement and had little patience for laziness, either physical or mental. He was very disciplined in his habits, did many chores around the house on weekends, always paid all the bills on time every month, and paid attention to exercise, especially tennis. Dad loved classical music, especially opera. He had a fine singing voice and once commented that he would have loved to pursue a career as an opera singer, but knew he probably wouldn't be able to support a wife and family doing this. But he would listen to opera on the radio, go to symphony concerts, and collected a huge library of classical music recordings, loving it when stereo superseded hifi. He read widely and involved himself in community affairs and his church. He was a leader in the Pittsburgh chapter of The United World Federalists, a group that actually believed in a form of world government that would go beyond the United Nations in terms of keeping peace. Dad didn't care that the organization proved to be far ahead of its time (and, sadly, still is). Dad was too realistic to be a pacifist, but he was a man so appalled by what happened in World War II that he felt he had to work on something that might prevent wars in the future.

So Bob Mann was smart and committed and accomplished; he had earned much of what he had, and he had planned well for a comfortable retirement for himself and his wife, prudently setting aside plenty of funds. For him, the loss of mental capacity, and thus loss of control and autonomy, was an intolerable prospect.

The above is only a very brief snapshot of my father's life and who he was. He was all of this, and so much more, until around the age of eighty. One day, vacationing with my parents in the Poconos, I asked Dad if he'd like to see my new laptop computer and what it could do. To my surprise, he said, "No, I'm not interested in that," immediately and firmly. Until then, he'd always been intensely interested in technological innovations. Now, he instead switched the subject to the squirrels he was counting on the deck, an increasingly engaging pastime. About a year later, when my parents were visiting me in San Francisco, Dad was clearly confused. At lunch one day he made mention of my first husband's name as the husband of my much younger sister. It was more than simple forgetfulness, and it was frightening to me because Dad seemed so radically mixed up. We did lots of walking up and down the notoriously steep streets, with Dad in the lead, probably priding himself on what good physical shape he was in. But on a bus tour of the city, in response to our guide's avalanche of information about the city's history, geography, culture, and architecture, Dad asked no questions. Normally he would have been engaged, curious to know more. Instead he rode silently, and then, very strangely, he began to hold forth about his hometown, Pittsburgh, reeling off facts and figures as if he were now the tour guide. It was embarrassing for us, and off-putting for our guide, but at the time, I thought little of it. On another evening, when all three of my sons joined Mom and Dad and me for a dinner in Chinatown, Dad embarrassed us further by making fun of Chinese people as we walked through the neighborhood by mimicking the sound of their language loudly enough for folks to overhear, and continuing this behavior even as we sat around the table. We politely changed the subject during these odd displays of prejudice, but I well remember how out of character they seemed.

Back at home, things got worse. Dad began ignoring stoplights on his daily walks around the neighborhood, scaring motorists. He would go into a local bar and pizza place at three o'clock in the afternoon and have two rum and cokes. Worse than that, after a lifetime of moderate drinking, he would get embarrassingly drunk at parties, hugely upsetting our mother. He would indulge in Tourette's syndrome-like profanity while alone in the kitchen washing dishes. He would ask my mother the same question, such as, "When are we having lunch?" every few minutes. When he arrived at my son's wedding, he looked around and asked quizzically, "I see someone in white over there—is that a bride?" He was less and less clear about what was going on, and talked very little, except to my mother when they were alone, perhaps realizing at some level how impaired he was. He stopped doing crossroad puzzles; he stopped reading. He became incontinent, causing horrific, mortifying situations.

Dad became confused about the insulin he was to take daily for diabetes, and it was this confusion that finally led to his move to a nursing care facility where he would die, four long years later. It was Thanksgiving weekend, and two of my brothers and a sister-in-law and I were in Sewickley for the holiday. Thanksgiving dinner had been rather chaotic. To give a young nephew something to do, we asked him to direct each person from the buffet table to his name card on the table. For fun, Jacob, the nephew, wanted to march each person around the table twice before landing at the assigned seat—fun for him, but confusing and frustrating for my father, who refused to play. We eventually all got seated and ate, but the next evening was a turning point. The plan was to go out to a nearby restaurant, but just as we were leaving, Dad grew very faint and pale and broke into a sweat. We realized it was something to do with diabetes, and Mom ran for the little gadget that could test his blood with a finger prick to see if he needed insulin or sugar. To get this wrong could have been disastrous, and in her anxiety, Mom fumbled with the pricker, hurting Dad, so that he cried out, while we all hovered around offering unhelpful suggestions as to what was needed. Eventually we took him to the hospital, just five minutes away. And there, they not only corrected his blood situation, but admitted him for tests and observation. That night, I slept in his bed next to my mother's bed. I didn't know it then, but the night before had been my father's last night at home, alone with my mother and me, his first little family.

Finally, after several days, the hospital diagnosed Dad with Alzheimer's disease and advised us he should no longer live at home, that his care would be too difficult for our mother. And so, my brother and sister explored several places and finally settled on Canterbury Place, a fine facility in Pittsburgh, half an hour from my mother, only fifteen minutes from my sister, with two levels of care for Alzheimer's patients.

Dad moved through both units, increasingly confused and non-communicative, no longer himself. Sometimes he thought Mom was his sister, sometimes he introduced one of the other patients to Mom as his wife. He was usually docile and seemed glad to see us when we visited. He liked going for rides in the car and going to the piano room and hearing me play. Sometimes he sang songs he knew, such as the Cornell *Alma Mater*. He travelled the corridors in a wheel chair, holding a clipboard and telling the staff he was making his rounds, usually in the middle of the night. Once, when an attendant was unlocking the coded door for us to go out, he commented under his breath, "Cunt!" This was the man who had chided me for using the word "hell" in front of him once, when I was eighteen! Four years went by in a steady decline: a broken leg, no more walking, bedsores that wouldn't heal. He didn't know any of his family, except sometimes our mother, and his confused, brief words could hardly be considered communication. The dad we had known and loved had died.

He had indeed lost his mind, and I am absolutely positive that when he was well, he would have asked us to help him escape from the abyss he now inhabited. I believe he would not have wanted to stay alive for at least the last two years of his life, maybe more. But we could do nothing—or, at least, that is what we thought. Canterbury Place would not permit withdrawing insulin because his diabetes was a pre-existing condition, but then they did agree to not replace his pacemaker battery, even though he'd had that when he was admitted. In hindsight, I wished we'd asked many more questions about these policies and why these distinctions were made.

Finally, on January 22, 2004, five years after his confused behavior in San Francisco, Dad died of pneumonia, alone, very early in the morning.

Three days later, we gathered with our own families, our mother, and her Presbyterian church full of friends to celebrate Dad's life. We sang his favorite hymns, our mother squared her shoulders and stepped confidently to the lectern to read a psalm, something she loved to do, and one of my brothers and I offered some reflections. These were mine:

And so, the final dregs of grief are now ours to drink. The long dying is over. The Bob Mann, the Dad who was, left us years ago. But Thursday morning early, when Mom called, the tears came again; the loss came fresh and shattering. The relief we'd hoped for was there too, but for me, unexpectedly wrapped in more grief—this final letting go.

There has been a big hole in our lives for a long while in that place where Bob Mann loomed so large, as husband, father, grandfather, and great-grandfather (though he never knew it), good citizen, serious Christian. That man left us back in the 1990s, and now the Dad he has been is gone, too.

But with this passing, we can celebrate his life, and draw close to one another and to him as we laugh and cry together in remembering, telling stories, holding Dad in the resting place of our hearts.

I loved Dad unreservedly, despite his flaws. He was my sire and my moral compass. He shaped my sense of humor and my love of music and my attraction to Christianity, which led to the work I now do. I think of him as shy and reserved, but even as little kids, we knew him as an affectionate tickler and roughhouser. Remember the "big boogie-bindo" and "pig piles"? They are as much a part of my memories as all of the volunteer, civic, and charitable contributions you read about in the paper.

Dad believed that people, and the world, are not stuck, that they can become better. He believed world peace was a real possibility, and he worked for it. He was not naïve, but he was an idealist—a serious Christian, as I said—a man who lived in hope.

Recently I came across a letter Dad wrote to me some thirty years ago when it seemed my life was coming apart. He said he wished I'd found a church that could help me, as this one had helped him. He said going to church helped him keep the promises he'd made to mother and to the church, kept him from being, as he put it, "as mean as I otherwise might have been." A few years later, I did find a church, and it has made a huge difference—and, even though it was an Episcopal church, Dad was thrilled!

Today feels somber to me, sad in the way important things are when they end, but the time had come. His life was long and happy and worthy despite these last few years. Dad—we've gathered to say our formal good-byes. There've been many already as we lost pieces of you, and one for me just a couple of weeks ago when I sensed I'd not see my father alive again. As I finish this public good-bye, Dad, I'll say what you so often said when parting from one of us: "Don't take any wooden nickels."

Amen.

Through those sad last years, the disconnect between the person Bob Mann had been and the almost non-person he'd become had loomed. We children spoke of "the Dad that was" and "the Dad that is." We had not known what to do; we had disagreed about whether he was somehow content in his diminished condition, about whether there was anything more aggressive we could do to hasten death. Our brother, Tom, actually considered taking him to Oregon where he would have had a legal right to die. And through it all, I felt I had betrayed my father by not being able to honor his wish to not go on living once he had reached a state of advanced dementia.

Dad's story is one that is playing out with increasing frequency as more and more and more people live longer and develop Alzheimer's or other forms of dementia. In my working life as an Episcopal priest, I made frequent visits to old and sometimes demented parishioners, living out their days in nursing homes. For the patients with dementia, these homes were like warehouses for bodies whose personhood was reduced to the most basic physical needs and incoherent utterances. Many were in far worse shape than my father ever was, and for a longer time, sitting propped in chairs, heads back, mouths hanging open, staring blankly as days, weeks, months and years unfolded. Their existence was an ongoing tragic slog for those who loved them, and their deaths came mostly as a blessing. Finally, the person who had been lost long before and was already missed and mourned, could be bid a final farewell—a relief for all concerned, as it was for our family and me.

FOUR

Caregivers: A Quandary of Compassion

My consideration of the issues confronting those facing advanced dementia and those who will care for them has included reading articles, books, news clippings, and letters to editors, but it has also included interviews and ongoing personal relationships with at least a few people who have been wrestling with the actual daily routine, or its many disruptions, that is life with Alzheimer's. Their stories, which so fully illustrate the quandaries faced by those charged with caregiving, or to whom this responsibility falls, bidden or not, are given here (and, again, their names have been changed, except as noted, to protect their privacy).

Family Members

Perhaps even more than patients, family members are the group most affected by questions about aid in dying. It is they who endure the cruel, slowly inevitable decline of a loved one and they who feel a responsibility to be faithful to what they think their relative would want, even as those wishes become more and more impossible to determine except from previous conversations. Family members must arrange for the financial support of their loved one, and this may involve draining away resources that could have gone for education for grandchildren, or security in their own old age. Family members, particularly children and spouses, may have a terribly hard time helping someone they love to end her life. And because financial concerns may be very real, guilt about these choices may add to their pain. It is this group for whom the idea of, or request for, help in ending a life in the face of impending death is perhaps the most painful.

Zoe Fitzgerald Carter's 2010 book, *Imperfect Endings*, recounts such a struggle. Her mother had clearly asked Carter and her two sisters to be with her and help in ending her life if and when her Parkinson's disease advanced to a certain stage. The sisters' lives are turned upside down. They hate the prospect of losing their mother. They worry about the legality of supporting her wishes. Added to that, their somewhat mercurial mother keeps changing her mind about the best time for her "exit plan." Not only do the sisters argue at various times with their mother about timing, but they are also divided about whether they can participate. In the end, after an overdose of morphine fails, their mother stops eating and dies after some days. The book well describes the kaleidoscope of feelings each daughter experiences. In the end, the summons to be with their mother as she surrenders her life brings a jumble of sadness, reminiscence, healing, impatience and frustration. Carter accurately portrays her family's reactions to a loved one's desire to end her life, and she sensitively limns the emotional as well as the logistical territory traversed in such a passage.

I have found among families I've talked to a broad spectrum of how their stories play out, and know there are no easy answers for how to live through or live out the devastation that advanced dementia can bring. I have certainly not found among these people any clear consensus about aid in dying, and many families do not want to discuss or consider it. For most, but not all family caregivers, the idea of requesting help in ending a life, even in advanced Alzheimer's, is painfully difficult. The concept is easier in the abstract where this aid can be viewed as a way of relieving suffering and honoring the express wishes of a dying person. But the reality of actually giving a pill, or a shot, or standing by for long days while someone you love no longer eats or drinks can be excruciating, and many tell me they could never do it.

I believe their reluctance to consider aid in dying could be overcome, but only under certain conditions. There would have to be preparation—honest conversations between husband and wife, parent and children, siblings. The person facing death would need to be absolutely clear in explaining why they would want to shorten the dying process and why assistance would be a loving act instead of a murder. There would have to be clearly written advance directives, discussed with family members before the dementia was at all advanced. All of this would be complicated by the fact that such assistance would indeed be deemed murder or illegal euthanasia in most of our states. And so the legal protection of these family members would be at stake. And so would the financial implications, especially in connection with any life insurance policies, which vary considerably and would need to be checked in each case. This can sometimes prove an almost taboo area for discussion, so great is the fear that monetary concerns would overly impinge on decision making. Tragically, too many families endure months and years of suffering that they ought to be able to avoid. The following are accounts of the experiences of various families with loved ones being slowly taken away by Alzheimer's. They illustrate the spectrum of difficulties that families face and the extent to which aid in dying is mostly not an option.

Gary and Joan

I had known Gary for years at the church where I worked. He and his wife, Joan, were very involved in the community; she had been the rector's secretary for years, while Gary had kept all the historical records and produced at least one history of the parish. They were fun and straightforward, respected by all. In 2009 Gary began to start forgetting "basic stuff," according to his wife. This was no surprise, really because his mother, grandfather, uncle and nephew had all had Alzheimer's. Even having gone through the disease with all these family members, or perhaps because of it, Gary very much desired to stay at home and not be committed to a care facility. Joan was in agreement. The couple had no children, but a nephew and niece lived next door, and the niece was a nurse, so it seemed that this arrangement could work. They availed themselves of several community resources. One was a daycare program for people with dementia where Gary spent two to three days a week from 9:00-5:00 for two-and-a-half years. There he would receive the stimulation of various activities geared for the functional levels of the patients. One of the best was the "Pal Program," in which people brought their dogs or other pets to interact with the clients. It also gave Joan the respite of free time away from the increasing demands of caring for her husband. The expense was daunting—$110 per day. The couple had no long-term care insurance, and eventually worked out a sliding scale for the fees that made them manageable, but the cost still had a huge impact on their retirement resources. Joan also joined a support group of other caregivers with whom she continued even after Gary's death.

One of the things Joan could still do with Gary, even up until a couple of weeks before he died, was to take him to church. They were well known and loved there, so it was fine for Joan to steer Gary around, looking vacant and confused as Joan propelled him to a seat. And when the music started, Gary joined in, still able to connect with music and actually sing the words of familiar hymns, especially Christmas carols.

According to Joan, the six years of tending to Gary were not grueling, and she never seriously questioned their decision to keep him at home. The idea of trying to shorten his Gary's life was apparently never addressed other than to give permission to the staff at the day care center to withhold extraordinary measures should a medical emergency arise. They didn't feel that hospice was an option as Gary was physically healthy, and Medicare doesn't cover such cases, so Joan and Gary just continued on with the help of their niece and nephew and loving friends.

During Gary's last months, things became a good deal more difficult as Gary would be up at night a lot, agitated and restless. Joan was afraid he would fall, and she knew he would be terrified if he woke up in a hospital. He didn't want to be bathed, but unlike many dementia patients, he wasn't violent or abusive to anyone caring for him. Joan hired a health care aid, first just for the evenings, but then around the clock, again, at her own expense.

Towards the end, Gary would repeatedly say, "I want this to be over," implying that he did have some idea of what was happening to him. Finally, in April of 2015, six years after his early symptoms, Gary died of pneumonia, at home in his bed. Joan, knowing I was a priest and lived close by, had asked me to come a few days earlier and offer Prayers for the Dying, a traditional rite in the Episcopal Church that they both valued. My sense on that day was that Gary was aware of my presence, or at least aware of the familiar words from *The Book of Common Prayer*, and he certainly seemed peaceful, not in pain, ready for the end.

Joan and Gary's story is one of the least harrowing I have encountered. When I spoke with Joan about her experience, after Gary died, she said, "I am more sad than angry." I believe her sadness was simply about what was being lost as the husband she knew and loved became less and less of the person he had been. She struck me as a strong and resourceful woman who was willing and able to honor and share her husband's wishes for how to manage his dying. She admitted they may have been in denial at first about what they faced, because even with having several relatives who had died of Alzheimer's, they just didn't consider any options other than keeping Gary at home, even as they struggled with how much help they needed and what they could afford. When I saw Joan in church a couple of months after Gary's death, she looked chipper and pretty, with new highlights in her hair and a lovely, colorful outfit. She had resumed some volunteer work in the parish office and said she was doing well.

In many ways, Gary's story is about as good as it gets, given what Alzheimer's can do. His dementia was not as extreme as some, didn't go on as long as some; he could stay at home, and his wife was not bankrupted. I felt, in my several meetings with Joan, that all my questions about aid in dying would be irrelevant or even unwelcome to her. She had helped Gary live his life to the end and had neither regrets nor bitterness about the ordeal. In my pastoral visit with Gary, I felt he was still there, still Gary, and in the tenderness of Joan and her niece I saw an enduring love and care that I respected and continue to admire. I feel aid in dying would probably not have been something this couple would have chosen or felt they needed, even if it had been available.

The Death of a Relative

My husband's father, J. William Flanders Sr., died in 1994 after only a couple of years of symptoms and about four months in a nursing facility. Bill Flanders Sr. was a southern gentleman from Dublin, Georgia, where his father had been the local sheriff for a time. But Bill made his way up north to Connecticut where he found a job with a large family construction company and a wife who was the boss's daughter. He flourished there, raised two children, Bill Jr. and Betty, worked hard for the family firm, loved golf and proved a kind, steady patriarch of a man. Not having gone to college himself, he must have been proud to send his son and namesake off to Yale, and he must have enjoyed being ushered into a world of art and music and cultural enrichment by his wife and daughter. When his son fell in love with a French girl while taking time off from college, it was hard for Bill Flanders, hard to make the long trip across the Atlantic for the wedding, fearing what to him seemed an exotic turn in his son's life. He weathered the trip, was immediately smitten with his pretty, young daughter-in-law and became the beloved "Poppo" of the eventual seven grandchildren his son and daughter produced.

His life was settled, serene and comfortable through his middle years, but then his wife died unexpectedly after surgery when he was eighty-one. Bill then married a younger woman friend, but the marriage didn't last and, after a polite divorce, he was on his own, living then in Florida. It wasn't long before the warning signs of dementia appeared. He became forgetful and confused; it was clear he shouldn't live alone. His son drove to Florida to bring his father back up north, and one night in the car, Bill Sr. became so disoriented by the oncoming headlights that he panicked and ordered his son to pull over. He just didn't know where he was; it must have felt like an alarming sensory overload.

For a couple of years, Bill lived with his son for half the year and his daughter for the other half, which worked pretty well. Each had a large house, and his daughter added an apartment to her summer home in Connecticut where Bill could have his own space but still be with the family. When he stayed with his son, Bill Jr. and his wife kept a close watch on Poppo, but once he almost got away. He made his way to a travel agency where he actually booked a flight back to Florida! Fortunately, the agent, noticing that Mr. Flanders seemed too old and confused to be traveling alone, and assuming he lived locally, found his son's number in the phone book and alerted young Bill. But overall, the family members supported this home care, and probably all benefitted from the presence of this kindly, somewhat dotty old gentleman.

Long before I married Bill Jr., I met Bill Sr. during a summer visit with Bill's sister when her father was staying there. He was sitting in a rocking chair on the porch, looking out over Long Island Sound, and he greeted me with utter gentility and courtesy, saying, "Hello, Susan, I'm very pleased to meet you." Then he said nothing more, but sat quietly as the conversations of the rest of the family swirled around him.

When home care no longer worked because of fears for their father's safety if left alone and issues of incontinence, Bill Jr. and Betty somewhat reluctantly placed their father in a local nursing care facility that had a locked ward for dementia patients. Clearly he hated this! He once attempted to climb up and over a wall surrounding the facility. Another time he threw a wheelchair through a large window, and another day, a flowerpot went flying—all this from a once gentle and kindly eighty-nine-year-old man who did not appear to have such strength. After these incidents, his sedative medicine was increased. But by then, he did not communicate much, didn't seem to know where he was or why, and barely knew his children when they visited. So one night, when the nursing home called to tell his son that Mr. Flanders had pneumonia and was being taken to the hospital, Bill Jr. and Betty not only rushed to the hospital, but called Betty's primary care physician and longtime personal friend and asked him to meet them there. He did, and he gave wise counsel. He cautioned them that if their father were admitted and treated for pneumonia, he would then be returned to the nursing home where the same scenario would probably play out in a few more weeks or months. The doctor told them that if one of them took him home, it would be just a few days before he would die fairly peacefully of the pneumonia.

After lengthy discussion, Bill and Betty decided to take him to Betty's house. Bill Jr. kept vigil on a mattress on the floor outside his father's room the first night. After that, with the help of a full-time nurse and some sedation, his father was kept comfortable and calm. Bill Jr. is a singer, and the nurse soothed his father with his son's CD's. After four days, Bill Flanders Sr. died in his daughter's home, with his son's music playing "Danny Boy," and the saga of his dementia came to an end.

To my mind, and to my husband's, this is a good story. Bill Flanders Sr.'s phase of late dementia did not last very long before he got pneumonia. He spent months, not years, in a nursing home. He was able to die at Betty's home, and no one had to assist in or cause this. Pneumonia was indeed, as is often said, "the old man's friend."

Daisy

Daisy has had Alzheimer's for ten years and is now in her late eighties. The onset of her disease was very slow, and she has had the good fortune of an incredibly loving and energetic daughter who has devoted herself to her mother's care and wellbeing. In doing so, her daughter, Angie, has also written and blogged widely about her experience and now gives talks regularly in churches and nursing homes about her experience. She has been clear and candid about the challenges she has faced and is facing, but is also unfailingly upbeat about the life she and her mother share. Her mother can now barely communicate verbally and doesn't really recognize many people any more, but Angie tells of the years of care almost as if she had been tending to the needs of a beloved child. She has pampered her mother with things she loves, like ice cream. She has arranged birthday parties and visits to church for her. She has kept her keen and loving antenna focused on everything that might make Daisy's existence in any way meaningful and pleasurable. She has downplayed whatever indignities attend Daisy's routines, using humor and playfulness to shield her mother from pity or the isolation some dementia patients face.

Although her mother is now in a nursing care facility, it is close enough to where Angie lives that she can visit almost daily, and she has found a program that provides a monthly subsidy for her care so that Angie finds it financially manageable. Angie recently lost her husband, but she still has the loyal support of family and friends in her crusade to make Daisy's life worth living right up until the end.

What I don't get in conversations with Angie is her perceptions about how and when the end may come. I don't get more than a rare hint of a dark, bleak outlook as the late stages of Alzheimer's loom. I don't get any sense that Angie would ever think her mother's life is not worth living. Although she doesn't say this, I think she feels that her own efforts can prevent this. And for all this care, this thoughtfulness, this selfless giving, I salute and respect Angie. I am struck by her energy—she looks neither tired physically nor beaten down emotionally from her role. I love this enthusiasm, and her outreach from her own experience to thousands of others.

I just wonder about how she and others will feel as late-stage dementia sets in and all her efforts to make her mother feel engaged and happy and loved may seem fruitless. I also worry that her powerful positive energy in the face of such a devastating disease may make others feel inadequate or not sufficiently caring, especially when they move their loved ones to nursing care, or, more poignantly, begin to wish, even secretly, for the mercy of death. Will others feel they haven't lived up to what Angie is putting out, this incredible mothering of her own mother; will they feel they are lacking in compassion? In my own conversations with Angie, I realized I didn't dare bring up the possibility of aid in dying; it seemed so far from the way Angie was dealing with her mother's dementia. I wish now that I had.

My concerns here are that the demands of dementia are so harrowing and so various that there is no one ideal response pattern. Caregivers can help one another; they can find support groups and read all the books and other material, but ultimately, each family faces this disease with its own questions, capabilities and resources. There is no "right" answer here, only what seems to be most faithful to who the patient was and is, and to what the caregiver/s can reasonably do to support that person. In these first cases no one was asking about aid in dying, and I wondered with each one, whether they even thought about it or would have chosen it had it been readily available. Perhaps I feared that in bringing up the option of aid in dying, they might feel I was judging the choices they were making.

A Walk on the Beach

My friend and I meet for our annual beach walk, making our way down steep steps onto the wide, smooth expanse of sand bordering Cape Cod Bay, within sight of Provincetown, its edgy bustle on the horizon. We are neighbors in Washington, DC but seldom see each other there; here in Truro, we meet every summer and sink into our comfortable rhythm: coffee first, including disgusted rants about politics, then a long, long walk as we calm down and catch up. We talk of our grown children, an upcoming wedding, a new granddaughter.

After a while, I ask my friend about her mother, whom I know has Alzheimer's and is in a care facility in Oregon. She sighs.

"Well, she's there, and she's well taken care of, but she doesn't know anyone, barely talks."

"Does she know you?" I ask.

"Sort of. Like, when I come and reach for her hand, she may have an idea of someone familiar."

"Can she still eat?"

"Oh, yes, she eats well and still feeds herself. But she's in diapers."

I tell my friend I'm doing some writing about the lack of options people have when facing advanced dementia and my interest in what can happen for people who wouldn't wish to live through the last stages of Alzheimer's or other dementia. We both comment on how valuable Atul Gawande's book, *Being Mortal,* has been in urging conversations within families and with doctors and other caregivers about end-of-life choices. And we lament how even in Oregon, where it is now legal for those with a terminal illness to choose to shorten their lives if they are of sound mind and go through the required protocols, there is no such choice for those with dementia. We have both found Gawande's description of how nursing homes and hospices and palliative care have developed, and serve as welcome alternatives to dying in ICU's or just in hospitals, to be helpful. But are these options sufficient when it comes to dementia? My friend remarks that her mother's care is costing $8,000 to $9,000 per month. She and her brother and sister can manage this, but it is a huge drain on resources. My friend doesn't say this, but I imagine some of these funds could be helpful to her son as he finishes graduate school and plans for marriage. Is this kind of money well spent in keeping a body going when she has so little capacity to engage with life at a level beyond the most basic physical functions?

Without trying to pin my friend down, because I think it may be intrusive to actually ask her if she would prefer it if her mother's life could be ended, I speak more generally about what her mother might have wanted while she could still communicate, and what her siblings hope for. Clearly there is disagreement. One sibling thinks the mother is still enjoying life and is content, comfortable, and even happy. The other is distant, not really involved, doesn't address these questions. My friend also pretty much detaches except during her visits every few months, waiting for the disease to take its course.

We've walked our two miles, and we head back up the beach. I think maybe my friend is tired of talking about this, perhaps because our conversation seems to go in circles. It seems now that there's nothing to be done, and the mother continues on as her children and caregivers try to make her life the best it can be. If anything could have been done, it would have involved a lot of honest conversation years ago at the onset of the disease and some clear articulation of the mother's wishes as well as understanding and agreement from her children to support her in whatever these were. But now it is too late; Atul Gawande's plea cannot be answered here. My friend and her family soldier on, waiting for death to come in its own time. We climb the steps to the house and cast a lingering gaze out over the beauty of the Bay. Maybe by next year, something will have changed.

Mercifully, by the next summer, my friend's mother did die, and we spent our walk talking about how the beauty of the service in their local Episcopal Church was so meaningful and consoling to my friend, how it honored and celebrated her mother's life. It was an ending, a welcome farewell.

Sacrificial Care and Its Burdens

I've recently finished a puzzling, saddening book, *Slow Dancing with a Stranger* by Meryl Comer. It is the story of a brave, intelligent and courageous woman who gave of herself unstintingly out of love, as do many others. It traces her struggle over more than twenty years to care for her husband on her own and to keep him at home and alive through all the terrible stages and ravages of the disease. His Alzheimer's was diagnosed early, in his fifties, while he was still in his professional prime as a scientist, but it took several years to even get a diagnosis. He hid his symptoms, denied them and refused assessments at first, and his wife went along, helping to shield him and worrying about his career being destroyed. Even some of the doctors they saw colluded in denying the onset of dementia, blaming stress and fatigue and "normal" aging.

Once the Alzheimer's diagnosis was finally given, Comer threw herself into first fighting and then coping with her husband's condition with everything in her. At first, this seemed admirable to me. I understood her desire to keep him at home, especially after various unsuccessful attempts to place him in a care facility; he was strong, often verbally and sometimes physically abusive, and several places would not keep him. The wife gradually developed a "care team" at their home, and she was always on the night shift, taking a full share in all the intimate care involved—bathing, toileting, repeated changing of clothes, wakeful spells.

Over time she got less and less sleep, but still she persisted, finally at the expense of her own rewarding professional life. Her one son and his family and a few close friends offered solace, but she became increasingly withdrawn, exhausted and drained, neglecting her own physical and spiritual wellbeing to an alarming extent. And all of this continued, worsening slowly, over twenty years! Twenty years of devoting herself to the well being, if it could be called that, of a man who eventually didn't know her, or anyone, couldn't speak, could barely move, really couldn't express himself in any meaningful way. At the end, the author's mother also became ill, and she took on the caregiving role with her as well!

As I read through this horrific saga, I wondered whether the author would at some point mention the possibility of some kind of end-of-life assistance, and whether or not she and her husband had ever talked about end-of-life scenarios once he began showing clear signs of dementia, or, better, even long before. Had they ever discussed how they saw their future playing out? I wonder if they felt they had good reasons for choosing the course they took, whether they felt they had options other than to let the trajectory of dementia play out, allowing the patient to stay at home and his wife to be the prime caregiver. I realize that back when he was in the early stages, there had not been nearly as much discussion in our society about end-of-life decisions, and that there was much more stigma around "assisted suicide" than there is now. But even so, I found it both poignant and troubling that Comer never acknowledged that she'd ever thought about whether ending the ongoing loss of her husband's brain might actually be a mercy. I wish I knew more about why this couple faced the long hard road of dementia in ways that seemed to yield no benefit other than prolonging bodily life for the husband. I wish I knew why this woman felt that utterly giving herself over to her husband's care at the expense of her own physical, spiritual, and professional health was worth it. Or maybe she and at least some of her readers may feel that her story was a noble one, the ultimate in self-sacrificial caring.

Much of her distress was channeled into fiery advocacy for finding a cure, finding ways to delay the onset and slow progression of Alzheimer's, and this is admirable; even if it couldn't really help her husband, it may well help others. Comer admitted many times that her husband had lost his personhood, that he was no longer the man she married, was no longer even a man who had any idea of who she was or ability to express or receive love. His eyes were blank; his face was empty of expression except for occasional upset. His life was reduced to a series of bodily functions, most of them managed only with great difficulty by his wife and her helpers. Despite their best efforts, dignity for this tall, handsome, intelligent man was long gone.

I felt sad about this woman's life, because in my mind, she too had become a victim of the disease, and I felt there was a whole category of questions that she and her husband had never addressed or hadn't known how to. I wondered why. I wondered if they had ever heard of Dr. Kevorkian? She did mention her horror when someone wrote to her about a method of causing death using a sealed plastic bag filled with helium over the head. I wondered if she had talked to people at Compassion & Choices, the organization working to make aid in dying more widely legal? Was she familiar with VSED (Voluntary Stopping of Eating and Drinking) as the one legal method of ending one's life or helping someone to do it? I cannot be sure, but given Ms. Comer's devotion to her husband and his care, and her passion to support advances in Alzheimer's research, she, and likely her husband, didn't consider aid in dying to be an appropriate option for them.

Comer's book is a striking example of the choices people make to navigate the long journey into advanced dementia, and for the author it was an all-in endeavor. Although she managed to continue her career, she ran herself ragged, physically and emotionally. The financial impact was huge, and she could never have cared for her husband as she did had her resources been as limited as most people's are.

For myself, I wonder whether her own agonizing struggles were worth the semblance of human life she was protecting. Her story is perhaps that of many who never once look towards the death of a loved one, even one with severe dementia, as a blessing, a relief. I want to be compassionate in the face of such a tragic situation, and here we are confronted with a fundamental question about compassion itself: What is compassion, for the patient and for the caregiver, as the slow withdrawing of all that makes us human unfolds? Is acceptance of advanced dementia an affirmation or a denial of the goodness and beauty of human life?

Sophia and Frank and Eleanor

It is another Saturday morning visit to Sophia. She is now living at a nursing care facility in northern Virginia that has a locked dementia wing, and I arrive full of curiosity and dread. Curiosity about how far along her Alzheimer's has progressed. Curiosity about whether I would want to be alive if I were in her shoes, about whether my father would have. Curiosity about whether Frank, her good, almost-Catholic-priest husband, ever wonders about whether it would be better for her or him if her life were to end sooner rather than later. Whether he even allows himself to consider questions about assisted suicide. Is all life sacred for him, always? Curiosity about what helps him bear up so calmly, and what it is like for him to come back here after a respite trip to Florida. I wonder if I'll ever have the courage and tact to approach him with some of these questions.

My dread is subtler, more buried beneath my questions. I dread encountering once again the ravaged shell of a formerly highly intelligent, articulate person; I dread the experience of my father all over again. I dread the helplessness and hopelessness that I will feel, and wonder if Frank feels it too, and I dread all of my own outrage that in the face of this loss of mind and personhood, there seems to be no compassionate, legal way to end such devastation.

When I first met Sophia, back in the 1980s, she was a nationally recognized author in the Episcopal Church and other protestant religious circles. With a degree from Union Theological Seminary in New York and years of experience as an active laywoman in the church, she was highly regarded for her work on church development and growth. She was well versed in Jungian theory and wrote widely about the connections between this and the paradox and ambiguity that can be hallmarks of sophisticated Christian faith. Sophia in those days was a lovely, dark-haired, curvaceous woman with bright, sparkling brown eyes and an infectious liveliness. She was a great source of wisdom for me when I was starting out as a new priest at St. Mark's Church on Capitol Hill. With women only recently having been ordained in the Episcopal Church, male and female clergy teams often found it awkward to establish collegial relationships. There was the excitement and spark and sometimes even sexual chemistry of working together, and there were also temptations to blur boundaries. Sophia not only wrote a book about this, but was also a keen observer and counselor to me as I made my way at St. Mark's. We formed a lasting friendship, even though Sophia had to speak some very direct and honest words to me some years later when my desire to become rector at St. Mark's put me at cross-purposes with that parish and its transition processes. I can remember her direct gaze and steady voice saying, "Susan, I think you have to realize here that your own needs and desires are in conflict with what is best for St. Mark's. You need to accept that." Words that hurt, but words that helped, and I've never forgotten them. I was pastor to Sophia and her first husband, Mike, as he suffered and died of cancer during those years, and our friendship continued after I moved to another church. Sophia went on to remarry, very happily and zestfully, and she and Frank were a shining example to all who knew them that sex and romance don't always end in older age, but can still flourish.

And then, some years later, I learned that Sophia had been diagnosed with Alzheimer's. By then I was retired and back at St. Mark's where Sophia still attended services, and my first encounter with her then was a shock to me. All the sparkle and keen intelligence were gone. She was a frail, small, grey-haired woman with a vague, confused look on her face. She needed to be guided around and watched during the service lest she wander off and not find her way back. I couldn't be sure that she knew me. She looked beseeching, wondering, hoping for clarity, going through the motions of church.

Her disease progressed until Frank could no longer care for her at home and she came to Woodside, a care facility in suburban Washington, DC. I asked Frank if I could come and visit for two reasons. One was that Sophia had been a faithful friend to me when I was forging my way as a priest. The other was my desire to follow the progression of her disease and how she and Frank managed as it invaded and took over their lives. I wanted this occasional glimpse, an hour or two every couple of months, to ground my own thinking about Alzheimer's and its tragic toll.

So, on this morning, I come to the room, cheery, a kiss on the cheek for Frank, a more cautious kiss for Sophia, as she probably doesn't recognize me. She is nicely dressed; the odd red hat she had on the first time I visited is gone. Her breakfast is brought to a small table in a sunny alcove where we all three sit. Frank and I make small talk, with occasional asides to Sophia who addresses her breakfast. She throws the bacon on the floor, muttering, over and over, "This will kill me, this will kill me!" We laugh, and Frank picks it up. She eats her eggs very fast, dropping bits on her dress, and then works on the sausage with her hands. She stops for a long while, looking at us quizzically, noting my earrings and saying that she used to have some.

According to Frank, earrings are not allowed here. He is sorry that Sophia is at Woodside, now forty-five minutes away from his home, although much closer to her daughter. Before, he could visit her daily, and they would go to McDonalds.

"McDonald's?" pipes up Sophia. "Can we go there now?"

Frank hesitates. "I did see one around here…maybe another time."

Sophia returns to breakfast, now gobbling some pancakes hurriedly, stuffing two or three bites in at a time, while Frank and

I continue our attempts at conversation. Sophia pulls up her dress and tugs at her diaper, and Frank casually remarks that it's a thick one today. I find I'm not particularly embarrassed; this is just the way Sophia is now—uninhibited, simple, sometimes lucid, mostly not.

We decide to go for a walk around the facility. This means moving Sophia from her chair at the table to a standing position in which she can use her walker. She cannot do this on her own, and when Frank tries to lift her, she resists and cries out that it hurts. Frank tells me he has a trick for this, and tells Sophia he wants to give her a kiss. Standing directly in front of her, he leans down and stretches out his arms, and she obediently bends forward and into his arms as he raises her face to his, and they kiss, and then hug, and then kiss again, and Sophia is on her feet. She clearly likes this, and it works beautifully. Bravo, Frank!

We walk down the corridors, passing the vacant faces of others, including a woman with a walker who goes along counting something: "There's one, there's two, there's three..." We pass a small exercise group of a leader and four patients. One does the leg and arm lifts; one slumps in his chair; one woman sits stiff like a ramrod, staring fixedly in front of her. A loud man with a huge grin introduces himself and welcomes us and tells us how much he likes it here and how he now has all new friends. Frank is polite and kind as they exchange names and shake hands. We make our way to the lobby where Frank wants Sophia to see the "birdies," lovely colored creatures flitting and twittering in their cage, but she has no interest. She says she wants to go back.

Finally we end up back in the small sunny room where there is a piano. I have brought some music, an *American Songbook* and sheet music for "Autumn Leaves" and "September Song." I enjoy playing through the latter two, but get little response. Once we turned to old favorites, such as "My Country 'Tis of Thee" or "Home on the Range," Sophia sings along as does Frank with his truly beautiful trained voice. It feels really good to all three of us to be doing something together, to see Sophia engaged. Is she happy? Do the words that emerge from the deep folds of past memory mean anything to her? I don't know. But I say a quick silent "thank you" to Carol back in San Francisco and to my dad, who both let me know that music is one way to sometimes pierce the veil of dementia and bring out some remembered words.

After a few more songs, I kiss my friends good-bye and leave with mixed feelings of relief and satisfaction. I know Frank has welcomed my company, and I guess Sophia has found it of some interest.

A month passes, and I visit Sophia and Frank again. Frank says she has fallen and has deteriorated cognitively as well. I don't really notice much difference.

She stares at me blankly: "Do I know you?"

"I'm your friend, Susan," I offer.

"You remember Susan from St. Mark's," says Frank.

"Do I know you?"

We three sit together. Sophia's gray hair, which used to be at least curled and nicely styled before she came here, is now cropped short and lies flat and lank against her head. Frank tells her she looks nice, and he and I exchange desultory comments. I gather up my courage and ask if he and Sophia had talked much about how things would play out once she got her diagnosis. Frank says they did, but he doesn't elaborate beyond saying they made arrangements for help with her care. We talk a bit about my memoir, and I promise him a copy, warning him that my theology is pretty progressive and that the book contains a two-page rant against the Roman Catholic Church. In a later email, Frank replies: "Hi, Susan. Enjoying your book so far. You're my most interesting friend-person-theologian-writer since Sophia!...and you make me think! or are you just feeding my 'paralysis of analysis?'...haven't got to your 'diatribe' yet...but I'm part way into some of your 'unusual' beliefs. You're certainly not boring! (though maybe a headache for some)." So if nothing else, I'm building a friendship with Frank based on our common interests.

This third visit continues much like the others. We go to the piano and I try to find old songs that Sophia might recognize and join in singing. I love playing and hearing Frank's voice, but after a few minutes, Sophia is no longer engaged and grows restless. I kiss Sophia and Frank good-bye and head to my car, guiltily feeling relieved and wondering how Frank will pass the rest of his time with his wife. I see them as trapped, and even though there is still clear affection between them, at least Frank knows things will only get worse. I don't know what Sophia knows.

Some weeks later, Frank emails me with a brief update: "I saw Sophia Sat. Took a while longer than usual to convince her of who I am... still likes to kiss me though!"

During each visit, I do an inventory of my reactions and feelings as I assess Sophia and Frank and wonder how things are for them. Frank did comment during one of my visits, "This is such a tragedy." I wonder again if they ever had conversations while Sophia was in the early stages of Alzheimer's about how things would play out. I resolve to talk further with Frank about his own hopes and fears and wishes about how things could go for Sophia. I hope I'll have the courage to ask him about aid in dying, even though we both know it would be illegal in their state and in the facility where Sophia now lives. I also worry that Frank's training in the Roman Catholic Jesuit tradition would make it almost impossible for him to entertain the idea of shortening Sophia's life. Why don't I suggest a time alone with him and ask him? Finally I put myself in Sophia's place. Would I still want to be alive at her stage of dementia? If I were actually in Sophia's place, perhaps my answer would be yes. As the person I am now, my answer is unequivocally "No!" I know others would have a wide spectrum of different answers, as would their caregivers, but for me, now, after yet another visit to Sophia, the answer is no.

Several months after my last visit with Sophia and Frank, I arrange to meet with Sophia's daughter, Eleanor, who lives near Woodside and is now Sophia's legal guardian. (Frank has actually divorced Sophia at this point in order to be with a female companion whose Roman Catholic scruples prevent her from being with a married man.) I had not seen Eleanor since her father's funeral, twenty years ago. She is vivacious, attractive, slender and blond, just as I had remembered her, and I was eager to get her perspective on her mother's situation. After a brief visit with Sophia, we settled in for lunch near the nursing home at a run-down sandwich place, which at least offered the quiet of a booth in which to talk.

Eleanor has a busy life. She is married with two young daughters, eight and ten, and works full-time in private practice as a clinical psychologist, and is now the primary family support person for Sophia. After briefly updating each other about the status of our lives, Eleanor was candid in assessing her mother's already bad and slowly worsening condition. Apparently, Sophia had endured some physical and verbal abuse at the first facility where she'd been, and that is why her daughter moved her, but she also pays for extra caregivers to attend to her. Fortunately, long-term care insurance helps to cover her mother's care, which costs some $7,000 per month. Eleanor says her mother barely knows her now and is extremely frustrated, bored, and confused about where she is or why.

"I know she's suffering," says Eleanor, "but there seems nothing we can do."

This was my opening to ask about aid in dying. "Eleanor, I'm not sure how you'll react to what I'm going to say, and I haven't dared to bring it up with Frank, but do you think about whether there is or should be a possibility of shortening or ending your mother's life?"

Eleanor's response was quick: "All the time! She would never want to be this way."

We then discussed the halting but steady progress of aid-in-dying laws in a number of states, and how none of them cover people with dementia. All require that the patient be of sound mind when requesting lethal medications, and so those with dementia who might seek death because of their dementia can't request it because of their dementia—a tragic "Catch-22," in which more and more people will find themselves. Eleanor was very interested in what I knew about aid-in-dying options, but she became intensely focused and attentive when I pointed out that stopping of eating and drinking (SED) was one legal way of ending one's life and that supporting someone in this was also legal, at least at home, if not in an institutional setting.

She actually began to wonder out loud, saying, "I could rent an apartment in the District [where an aid-in-dying law has just been passed], find someone, perhaps a nurse to help me, and stay there with Mom." But then she paused. "I don't want to end up in the clink either!"

I felt some alarm, as though I'd led her down a path a bit too abruptly, too quickly. I wasn't at all sure I wanted to be the person who persuaded someone to help her mother die, as strongly as I believe this is a good outcome for some demented people. I cautioned Eleanor to speak with a lawyer who specializes in care for the elderly and dying, and said I could supply her with a name.

And then we talked about what her brother would want, and Sophia's ex-husband, even though they were divorced by then. Apparently the brother is pretty much out of the picture, seldom sees his mother. Frank continues to visit Sophia, but less frequently. So complicated! Here I had set up this lunch just to get to know Eleanor a bit and feel out what she might think about her mother's plight and whether she had even considered the possibility of aid in dying, and here we were discussing specific possible plans to carry this out!

I think we both were a bit taken aback, and our conversation grew more general. I told her I would send her a very good article on SED from the Hastings Center, a bioethics research institute, along with other articles I thought might be helpful. However, as we talked, we both realized that the lack of clearly expressed written advance directives from Sophia at a time when she was capable of that would preclude even a process of withholding food and drink. Although Eleanor had wondered about shortening her mother's life and wished there were a way, this one possibility was finally not really feasible or legal. And the actuality of withholding nourishment gave her pause, as I believe it would give anyone. It had given me pause, too. What am I really advocating? Once the abstract becomes a real person, with real family members, there is much to consider, or re-consider.

Several months later, I visited Sophia again with Eleanor, who had warned me that her mother was much worse. Indeed she was. She was in bed and very small and thin. Her hair and even her skin were a dull gray. Sophia looked at us, but totally vacantly, responding with some slight muttering when her daughter took her hand and leaned down to kiss her. Eleanor and I chatted, looking at Sophia, trying to include her, but she wasn't in; she was out, not home any more. Some lovely music by John Rutter was playing, which reminded me that Sophia had loved his music. Eleanor asked if I would help plan and lead Sophia's funeral when the time came, to which I gladly agreed, and we talked about various music and readings that might be appropriate. I kissed Sophia good-bye when we left, thinking I might not see her again, hoping so. I was surprised to hear Eleanor speak with one of the caregivers about her mother's dose of Ensure, and I wondered to myself why that was being done. Wouldn't it be better for everyone if Sophia slowly stopped eating, and if death came sooner than with supplementary nutrition?

It just seemed crazy to me, a surreal setting in which someone has lost almost everything that makes her human, and yet huge amounts of time and money are expended to keep her alive, keep her company, keep her stimulated—why? She wouldn't want it; her daughter doesn't want it; her former husband doesn't want it, and in fact has exited for a new life.

I suppose the people at Woodside want it. It pays the bills and provides jobs tending to bodies that house wrecked minds and lost personalities; maintaining cleanliness and nutrition despite all loss of dignity; speaking cheerfully to those who have no more words and comprehension. These are very tough, boring and, I should think, unsatisfying jobs. We don't pay these people enough, and the amount of money we already do spend on these patients is an enormous drain of funds that could be used in so many more life-giving ways. It feels like a stuck situation. Patients and families are stuck; caregiving systems are stuck; and there seems to be no feasible legal way out. Is there nothing anyone can do but watch helplessly as Alzheimer's takes its long dreaded course towards an end that is a mercy, but that no one can hasten?

Sophia finally died in March of 2017. I had visited her about a month before that, and things were much the same. By then, her eyes were mostly closed. She seemed calm, and did turn her head towards her daughter when Eleanor greeted her. She ignored me. As we left, I kissed Sophia good-bye and was pretty sure that for me it would be the last time. A sense of loss washed over me, but it was very much from the realization of all that had already been lost, of the Sophia who had been friend and mentor and colleague to me, of the piece of my own history of which she had been so much a part. In terms of her imminent death, I felt only relief that she and her son and daughter would be free of this suffering, and that the Sophia she had become could now begin to be overtaken by the Sophia they remembered.

Several weeks later, I led the memorial service for Sophia in the church where both she and I had so much history.

Other Caregivers and Stakeholders

Along with family, several professional groups have a stake in end-of-life decision-making because of their roles. Doctors, whose classical version of the Hippocratic Oath commands that they "do no harm," must wrestle with what this means when aid in dying is requested. Nurses also confront the meaning of their profession as caregivers, according to their own sense of duty. Lawyers must inform and counsel patients and family members about the legal and moral implications of seeking death in the face of advanced dementia at a time when our country does not yet allow for it. And, clergy are often part of conversations with patients and family members who are caught between what they most want at the end of life and what they feel to be God's will or at least what they deem to be a faithful response in this devastating situation. They want to know what love demands, and many worry about what might happen after death, and so they turn to clergy for spiritual guidance.

Physicians and Nurses

Agency has huge moral valence in cases of aid in dying. Doctors, who are sworn to be healers, may often object to being agents of death and should never be forced to do so. But, as doctors are those most likely to be asked to help a person end his life, it is important to understand their concerns and to recognize that doctors, as well as nurses, can vary widely in their willingness to provide aid in dying.

Bob

I sat down with Bob, a primary care physician I know well, and asked him about his experience with patients who wanted him to help end their lives. Settled comfortably in his office decked out with baseball mementos, we fueled ourselves with coffee as I raised my questions. He had indeed faced some cases, and he told me about them candidly. In each case, he had responded to the specific request of the patient or a family member and expressed no legal qualms about these actions.

He wrote a prescription for thirty Nembutal, a common sedative, for the son of a lung cancer patient. The son opened them to produce about two tablespoons of powder, made a slurry with some fruit juice and gave it to his mother, who drank it along with a shot of vodka. Bob gave her a shot of valium.

He aided two other patients in dying. A judge who had prostate cancer that had recurred and spread had decided with his wife to end his life. Bob provided the same assistance as above. And last year, he helped a ninety-six-year-old who had had dementia for years and was beyond bedridden, at home, "a complete vegetable." The doctor got a tank of helium from a party store and tubing from a hospital and used these to bring about suffocation. He told me it "took too long" (about thirty-six hours) and feels that the Nembutal is a better method.

I asked if he sees himself as a doctor on the liberal end of a spectrum on aid in dying. Bob says he's on the left, but not the most extreme end. He feels that in these situations, it's "the kindest thing you can do." He said that in the "old school" of medicine, the mantra was "where there's life, there's hope," but then questioned that philosophy in the case of a massive stroke, with no possibility of recovery. Here was a person in the ICU with all kinds of tubes going in and out, and he felt it was "cruel" to participate in keeping that person alive. Bob just doesn't see it as his job to keep people alive as long as possible, even if healing is the heart of his profession. He cited an accountant friend who had very rapidly advancing Alzheimer's and ended up in a local nursing home where he had to be restrained and heavily sedated. This friend was given liberal morphine and his last day was peaceful.

My doctor friend finds it a great irony that although his patients tell him the thing they most fear about aging and death is "becoming demented," their advance care directives seldom include anything about this. And so we talked about whether any advance care directives involving aid in dying for an advanced dementia patient could be legally honored, given that the person would be unable to make a decision at the point they would want the directive to be followed. Bob's aunt suffered dementia for thirty years and was eventually "like a carrot." Based on all his experience, he feels strongly that advance directives could and should be extended to include aid in dying for the severely demented.

But Bob also offered another perspective. "At the risk of being cynical," he pointed out that "nursing homes have an economic interest in having lots of demented patients who require long stays, and eventually minimal maintenance." He sees this as analogous to the economic benefits to for-profit prisons, which need inmates.

These needs can affect our policies on both aid in dying and on crime and punishment. He continued, saying that "if politicians could be even momentarily honest," they would face these issues, and they would recognize the commonly known statistic that about half of our health care costs are incurred during the last year of life. And another pertinent statistic is that Alzheimer's is the most expensive of all terminal diseases because of the lengthiness of its course.

Bob summed up our conversation with his strong recommendation that we develop more objective criteria for use in advance directives, including those for dementia patients, and that we recognize the economic impacts of such policies.

Bruce

I was also able to spend time with Bruce, a doctor of internal medicine. He is seventy-six, retired and living on the coast of Maine, where we sat and talked in wooden armchairs gazing out over the rocky shoreline one foggy morning. Bruce mentioned the Euthanasia Education Fund, which presented the pros and cons on the issue for physicians, and was a forerunner of the Physicians for Compassionate Care Education Foundation (PCCEF), which opposes physician-assisted suicide. Bruce was clear that, as a physician, it would be hypocritical for him to prescribe lethal medication, nor would he administer a lethal dose. But he would be OK with a patient finding someone to do this and would willingly "protect the comfort and dignity" of a dying person and not try to cure or prolong survival in the face of natural death. Bruce suggested that "Allow Natural Death" (AND) is a good alternative to "do not resuscitate" (DNR). To institute this, a person should say, while still of sound mind, that they don't want any interventions done to keep them alive, once they are in a terminal state, and, with dementia, once certain key elements of personhood no longer existed.

Bruce well recognizes there may be a tension between what is seen as comfort care and life-saving measures. Are food and drink included here? Bruce would accept gradual tapering off of nourishment; if the patient can't feed himself, he should be fed, but only for a time, and not in endless attempts to provide a certain amount of calories. This gradual decrease would lead eventually to system breakdown and death, and Bruce would support this.

He stresses that it is essential, in planning for a natural death or legal aid in dying, that a patient speak directly to all close family members and not just communicate via one, such as a spouse or a child, what his wishes are for end of life. These should also be written down and shared with all relevant family members. This awareness on the part of all involved is also helpful, if and when a natural death is allowed or any legal means are employed to hasten death, in avoiding both arguments about what the patient really wants, and guilt trips such as, "Didn't you love your mother?"

Bruce mentioned that some people who wanted to be able to have their lives shortened had tattoos saying "DNR" inked on their bodies! Even that clear message was not always honored, he said, depending on whether or not the patient seemed "cadaverous" or obviously dying, in which case, the tattoo might be more compelling. He reminded me that it is always easier not to put someone on a ventilator than to take him off. A "temporary" use might be a better way of handling this. It would signal to patient and family that a situation was not sustainable over the long term and that recovery would not be possible.

Bruce reminded me that certainty is often not attainable in medicine; that's why we hear that medicine is still more art than science. We both felt the art of medicine is key in the relationship between a doctor and a patient with advanced dementia who could no longer communicate what he wanted. We wondered if previous directives and preferences, particularly for aid in dying, that had been laid out when the person was of sound mind, would be upheld legally. Currently, in all states that even allow assisted suicide, one criterion is that the patient be of sound mind at the time the assistance is requested. And so, the crux of the argument would be whether advance directives written years earlier, before dementia, would be honored once the disease had advanced and it was impossible to know what the patient then wanted.

Bruce brought up the psychological and spiritual aspects of aid in dying. Some people really do believe in miracles, and so, for them, there is always the possibility of healing. For some there is a stigma attached to suicide, and perhaps even more to euthanasia, and shame and guilt can surround even considering these attempts to shorten life. In Bruce's experience the role of prayer was a conundrum, a minefield. For those who believe prayer can bring about miracles, there is the problem of who gets cured. Many pray for healing; sometimes a person gets well and attributes it to prayer. But what about all the people who pray and don't get well? Is their fear and anxiety in the face of death compounded by guilt, that maybe they didn't pray enough, or not hard enough, or didn't have strong enough faith? Then there are those who don't pray at all, who don't believe in God, and yet some of them recover, seemingly miraculously. There is just no certainty. And for those who suffer advanced dementia, what can prayer possibly mean? The reassurance and comfort it can provide for those who pray and are prayed for might be out of reach, beyond what they can comprehend or recognize. Not that prayer is useless; it may certainly provide solace for caregivers, especially if they allow themselves to express the hope they may well feel for death to come and relieve both them and their loved one. Prayers can be a powerful way of expressing hopes and fears and gratitude, a focusing of spiritual energy. But to my mind, prayers that plead for a deity to cure disease or prevent death, or even to bring it about, are problematic and represent a wrong-headed idea about what faith and prayer are all about.

Finally, Bruce did say that although he would not participate in it, aid in dying is one of the few things that would both "decrease suffering and save money," but he felt there are serious slippery slope issues that would compound the other difficulties of legalizing this practice. One such issue is that family members might be influenced unduly by financial concerns, including their desire to protect an inheritance. Another would be that patients themselves would feel pressured to seek aid in dying, or guilt if they didn't, because of the burdens of their care on others.

Ted

I drove to the office of Ted, a long-time friend and former parishioner, and a psychiatrist. Both he and I had worked on memoirs, and we have kept in touch over the years. He was most interested to talk with me about the special problems of dementia patients in preparing for death, well aware that they are a special category when considering issues of assisted suicide and euthanasia. Dementia patients really don't fit into the various arguments for and against these decisions as do those who are of sound mind— and all current legislation applies only to those who are of sound mind at the time when the decision is made. Given this situation, he encouraged me in pursuing this debate and in being part of the larger conversation.

Ted doubts that what a person says or writes in advance when still in possession of his mental faculties will be honored years later when he has lost them. The claim will be made that the demented person is not the same person as the capable one, and might not necessarily make that choice at the time when he would have wanted to exercise it. Hence, something like a "dementia clause" suggested by Compassion and Choices might not hold up legally except if food and drink were withheld, which is at least arguably legal now. We agreed that for many people, steps that involve removing, withholding, or stopping treatment might be more acceptable ethically than any actual steps taken to end a person's life. But waiting for circumstances that would lead to such withdrawals could take years for a dementia patient with a healthy body, especially in cases of early onset of the disease.

Ted and I discussed the role of suffering, and the extent to which it might have value, especially if borne with grace and dignity. Problems here for dementia patients are that: a) they might not experience suffering (but their caregivers and loved ones would), and b) grace and dignity are two things of which dementia robs people, so they may have no capacity for either one, no possibility of being models of suffering bravely endured. But to the first point: the late stages of dementia often represent profound suffering to the person confronting them while they still have their mental faculties. The very idea and demeaning prospect of what they will become can induce profound suffering in the patient for long months and years until the disease takes that consciousness away, removing present suffering. But then again, how is it possible to know about any physical pain and suffering if a person has lost all capacity to communicate?

Del

Del Welch (her real name, used by permission) is a psychiatric nurse in Maine who has worked both in assisted living facilities and in home care. When she heard me preach a sermon about aid in dying for dementia patients at the tiny summer chapel in Tenants Harbor, Maine where I vacation every summer, she offered to talk to me about her experiences. She came to our house, and as a parade of sailboats entered and left the harbor in front of us, we plunged into our conversation. Del helpfully distinguished between home care, which she described as "what is needed if people can't get to a doctor," versus hospice care or in-home nursing care, both of which are usually shorter term (about two months for acute situations) and are usually covered by insurance.

Del described her experience with a colleague who had Pick's disease, another degenerative disease of the brain, which particularly impairs language as part of the aggressive dementia it causes. As her friend grew sicker, Del could no longer understand what he was saying, but his wife felt she could communicate with him to the end. This underscored for me how important the ability to speak is for most people as one criterion for making life worth living. However, it is really the deterioration of the brain that is decisive. For instance, patients suffering with ALS ("Lou Gehrig's Disease") often lose the ability to speak, but because their minds are still clear, they may live for quite a while in that state and consider it well worth being alive.

Del told me about an organization, Aging with Dignity, and its document (easily and affordably available online) titled, "Five Wishes." This document could be helpful as a family conversation starter and a more useful tool than the standard advanced directives and power-of-attorney documents because it addresses values and interests beyond just physical aspects of care. However, I didn't find anything about situations of advanced dementia in the Five Wishes documents. I called Aging With Dignity to see if they had any literature with such provisions. The somewhat flustered response from the chirpy young woman who took my call was, "Um...no."

Lawyers

Because laws vary across the country in regard to aid in dying, and because it is still illegal in most states, considerations of helping even a competent person end his life are fraught with moral and legal concerns, and much more so with advanced dementia. I was helped in understanding these issues in a couple of conversations with Ron Landsman (who was happy to have me use his real name), an attorney specializing in legal issues for the elderly. Ron has an infectious enthusiasm for analyzing moral dilemmas and a wise, seasoned approach to our human anxieties in the face of death.

We sat in a cozy corner of a Bethesda coffee shop, way too early in the morning, fortifying ourselves with coffee and flaky croissants as we faced the harrowing world of Alzheimer's patients and any end-of-life choices they may have. He noted that legal choice in dying includes suicide, even if some religious or other moral authorities condemn this. It is in going beyond suicide to assisted suicide where the real legal and moral problems and disagreements surface. He well recognizes that people will make foolish choices and that slippery slope arguments loom whenever assisted suicide is considered.

"This is a perfectly intractable case!" declares Ron, about the situation of those with dementia who might want to shorten their lives, because we have no way of knowing, when we are of sound mind, what we will want when we aren't. This catch raises a basic question about how we define "wanting," once our capacity to consider our quality of life, remember our previous wishes, and look ahead, is impaired or destroyed. Why, I wondered, can't our considered and expressed wishes while still of sound mind still stand after dementia takes over? Shouldn't we give those wishes and any directives written to honor them precedence over the confused, perhaps garbled, probably constantly changing desires we may express in late stages of dementia? Ron seemed to feel that this would be very tricky legally, especially if family members were in disagreement about what a patient wanted at the later time, even if earlier wishes had been understood. If people have a legal right to change their minds and the provisions of their wills and advance directives, don't they always have this right? But what if advance directives about dementia are prepared specifically to guard against such changes once a person is no longer mentally competent to make decisions?

Ron was hopeful that progress in aid in dying is being made and is spreading to more and more states. We both noted the rapid decline in society's opposition to gay marriage in recent years, which led to Supreme Court acceptance. The ban on smoking in public places and a growing general opprobrium of smokers is another example. Although neither of these involves the taking of lives, each illustrates the way an issue can accelerate rapidly in the public's eye once a critical level of acceptance is reached. Perhaps aid in dying might be like this; it might gain traction with increasing speed as support grows. Ron also wondered whether assisted suicide could be seen as treatment withdrawal. This would be different from administering lethal medications, but would it have the same legal and moral valence? And what about nourishment? Certainly that is not "treatment," but life-sustaining care; would it be legal to withdraw this if a patient were incapable of feeding herself?

To Ron, these questions skirt a more basic one: what kind of life is worth living? How do we value the self, and the kinds of relationships possible (or not) once dementia is far advanced? Do these patients still have a self? And how do we view suffering? Is there some intrinsic nobility in bearing pain and indignity and loss of personhood? Is there some point at which nobility is no longer a factor?

"Be very careful about advocating the nobility of others' suffering!" Ron commented as we finished our conversation.

Clergy

I have talked with many clergy colleagues about death with dignity for dementia patients. My basic question to each of them was whether they could support and even bless a person's decision to ask for aid in dying should they reach an advanced stage of dementia.

One Episcopal priest was open but cautious in his approach. He thinks this is very much a situational ethics dilemma, and would not feel comfortable in a support role unless there were clear advance directives. He then likened his position to that of a priest when people ask him to bless their marriage. In that case, several, usually three meetings, are held with the couple so that the priest can assess their readiness for marriage and their commitment to keeping their vows. He would want to talk with the person requesting aid about what values were prompting this request and how this decision did or did not reflect the person's faith. And, if the person were already seriously demented and incapable of such conversations, this priest would want to talk things through with the spouse or other next of kin to get as much clarity as possible about how the patient came to the decision to write the directives. The priest would want to explore the consequences of following through with aid in dying, and what this would mean to the caregivers and any others close to the situation. He also felt there was a distinction for him between his role as a pastor—to provide comfort and support—and the role of an ethical authority who might be more directive in urging one course of action or another.

In another conversation with a different clergy colleague, we talked about the contrast between discussing aid in dying in the abstract and thinking about it in terms of one's own life and partnership. He wondered if he could actually help a spouse die or participate in withdrawing nourishment, even if that had been the clearly expressed wish of the patient before dementia took over. We talked about the irony of situations where loved ones continue to urge extremely demented people to eat, even though they know that death would be a mercy and that the patient would not want to be alive in that condition. This brought up the question that has come up regularly in my queries about aid in dying: how can one possibly know what the severely demented person wants at the time? Is she still the same person who wrote the clear directives years before? Do you honor that person, or agonize about whether the person you're now dealing with should have agency?

Other clergy I talked to were not so open to aid in dying. It was frustrating to me that some seemed to confuse situations of obvious terminal illness, such as late-stage cancer, with the somewhat different timeline of dementia. Others claim that all life is sacred and so will have no part of aid in dying, no matter how debased a life can become with advanced dementia. They often struggle with current aid-in-dying laws even for those who have all their mental faculties. These clergy may feel torn between pastoral empathy and institutional orthodoxy. And wherever aid in dying is illegal, then some clergy fear that those who help may be in jeopardy of criminal prosecution.

These concerns have a bearing on real stories of suicide and aid in dying, thrusting us into a world of ambiguity and uncertainty, a world where questions of right or wrong are often more properly answered in terms of what is faithful, or what is loving? By what is faithful, I mean here a response that takes into account all the aspects of a specific situation and recognizes that there is no good answer that will cause no harm and satisfy everyone. A faithful response is one in which both the costs and promises of a decision are weighed, and people consider very carefully what values are in play. Usually there are a number, and so an answer that simply declares, "all life is sacred," is too simple.

With advanced dementia it is important to consider what the person would have wanted for their last years, what the illness has made of the person's life as it has taken over, and what the emotional and financial burdens of care do to the family. What is the kindest, most loving thing to do? As a pastor and priest, I see assisted deaths in these cases as actually honoring the value of human life by mercifully ending it when all that makes it human has disappeared in the late stages of dementia. Here the fundamental definition of what makes life human and worth living becomes a key factor. Here the questions of what a patient would choose now or would have chosen before become almost impossible to answer, either by the patient or anyone else, unless clear advance directives and honest conversations have happened much earlier, while the patient was still competent to express herself. But among my colleagues there is certainly not much consensus.

Over bowls of chili, I talked with Don, a clergy colleague, about a variety of terminal cases. Don had many anecdotes about end-of-life wishes including Do Not Resuscitate directives and palliative care and hospice. But none of them were about aid in dying with dementia. Sally, another priest, wanted to talk about "good deaths," where people were kept comfortable and pain-free, and were able to say good-bye to their loved ones and came to accept death as they faced that great unknown. This would not be the situation of advanced dementia patients, and our conversation never got beyond her "good death" concerns.

Many clergy hold a strong and reassuring belief that there is indeed a life after death with God, even if they can't articulate what that might be. I do not share that belief, nor can any of us possibly know. But given how so much of what we value about this life is long gone by the time someone dies of Alzheimer's, I would think hastening death would be considered a benefit for these believers, a speedier passage into "the nearer presence of our Lord," as some clergy occasionally intone.

I spoke with one fellow clergy member whose wife had had Alzheimer's and who had died almost a year before. I assumed that she had gone through the bleak late stages, but he was quick to tell me that she had died of pneumonia before that. He had no interest in talking about aid in dying; he just felt it was beyond what we should do in the face of the mystery of death, a kind of "playing God," and something he could never do.

In my conversations with other clergy, I worked out for myself at least one theological angle on the dilemma presented by advanced dementia. I addressed that dilemma in the sermon following, which is based on a central question in the Christian gospels: what does it mean to love one's neighbor as oneself? I have preached this sermon at several churches, and in each case it has yielded much feedback, mostly positive, although I imagine that those who took offense or were troubled may have chosen to keep silent. Parts of this sermon clearly are based on my own experience with my father:

"Love of God, Love of Neighbor: A Sermon"

[The Pharisees] gathered together, and one of them, a lawyer, asked [Jesus] a question to test him. "Teacher, which commandment in the law is the greatest?" He said to him, "You shall love the Lord your God with all your heart, and with all your soul and with all your mind. This is the greatest and first commandment. And a second is like it: You shall love your neighbor as yourself." On these two commandments hang all the law and the prophets. (Mt. 22:34b-40)

Today I want to talk to you about suicide and assisted suicide in the decline of old age. This is a matter that is much in my heart and mind, a matter that is cropping up increasingly in the media, in magazine articles, books, and in some lives we know about. It is a matter that demands our best wisdom and enormous compassion. It is also a matter of forethought and of thinking ahead and having important conversations; it is a matter of being prepared, and so, perhaps, there is a connection with today's Gospel.

I will frame the questions in the context of that encounter between Jesus and a lawyer who wants to know which is the greatest commandment, and Jesus's answer about loving God above all and loving one's neighbor as oneself.

And so let me tell a story, with Jesus as a present day character:

One day a lawyer came to Jesus, much troubled about his wife, Mary. She had been diagnosed with Alzheimer's four years ago when she was seventy and was now in the late stages of the disease. Mary was in a care facility because the daily demands of her care on him and their two grown children had finally become too great, and her ability to recognize and communicate with them had become too small. They had long since lost the woman they had loved as mother and wife, but her body was still with them, reduced to occasional sporadic motions and sounds, or to long catatonic silences. She was technically, chaotically alive, a pumping heart—but no self, no will or personhood. At the time of her diagnosis, Mary had given her husband a letter, which he now held in trembling hands as he stood before Jesus.

A few years ago, just after her diagnosis, Mary, fearing the exact situation she was now in, had written this letter to her husband and children. Despite early symptoms, she had actually put off writing for some time while the letter germinated in the humus of her soul, getting ready to sprout. The letter was about life and death and control and compassion and dignity and autonomy and being heard and understood—all of this, and it felt risky. And so Mary had delayed, waiting until experience dictated the writing, until her jumbled, frustrated, angry thoughts distilled into something almost vocational. She needed to be absolutely clear about what she was proposing and how it would be received, and whether it could be held in the realm of sacred love—love of life, and love of those who loved her.

She had known others who wished to shorten their lives as some terrible disease took over their bodies; she had had conversations with friends about what they would do if facing intractable pain or disfigurement or loss of dignity. She'd talked to people about dying on their own terms, being able to control the circumstances of their deaths. And she'd seen at least one friend diagnosed with early-onset Alzheimer's and watched with horror as the friend became a stranger to her and even to herself; she became someone she would never have wanted to be.

Then there were all the years of her own father's illness, marching by like the scenes in a Greek tragedy where the very wishes and intentions of even the most admirable characters are cruelly distorted, and the end most dreaded is exactly what happens. Mary's father saw his neighbor's dementia progress until he was taken off to a home, his wife exhausted, nothing left of the jolly friend across the street. He told his family he never wanted that to happen to him; if he lost his mind, he didn't want to go on living.

But he did lose his mind, first in little ominous hints that he tried to cover up and his family tried to not notice. Gradually, question after repeated question, dangerous walks against streetlights, embarrassing incontinence episodes and total confusion about diabetes medications led to his incarceration in a locked Alzheimer's unit. There he would be safe, taken care of and protected so he could go on living through four more years of life he would never have wanted. He was a sad, old child, not too sure who his wife or children were, packing his bags to go home, dribbling his food on his bib, lying passively in his diapers except for when he would try to escape by climbing the wall outside his room. Mary watched this unfolding denial of her father's expressed wishes. She held his hand and led him slowly down the hall when she visited, took him out for a walk where he might think the plastic bag fluttering in a tree was a bird, asking, "What kind of bird is that?"

Mary wondered if his insulin could be withdrawn, allowing him to die, but "That would be murder!" came the appalled, judgmental response.

Two more years went by, and Mary's and her family's prayers were for his death, even though his wife said she felt guilty about that. He broke his leg in a fall and could no longer walk. There were little songs at the piano in the music room. Mary had learned a special piece on the piano, a transcription of the lovely theme from Rachmaninoff's Piano Concerto No. 2. It had been her father's favorite. When she played it, he looked blank, but he could still sing, "Twinkle, Twinkle, Little Star." Gradually her father stopped singing or talking, stopped recognizing anyone but occasionally his wife, languished in bed until pneumonia finally came one January night when he was all alone. Mary's family gathered both to share the grief that had been on hold for years and to celebrate, finally, the end of an ordeal that need never have occurred.

As she navigated these introductions to the Alzheimer's that would eventually capture her, Mary did everything possible to learn about dementia and options for its victims. She read articles, novels, medical reports. She went to movies about dementia. She visited nursing homes where the bodies were stored, devoid of essential humanity, being tended more like plants, isolated and alone, with some families realizing that they didn't know whether they visited or not; it made no difference. Others had plenty of company, but there was no interaction, just going through the repetitive motions of conversation that was not; of affection poured out, often with no sign of being received.

Mary got angry. Mary missed no opportunity to speak at length about her growing conviction that victims of dementia should have a right to terminate their lives and to receive the help needed to do it at such point that those lives lost all semblances of dignity and human awareness. Some thought Mary was cold and unfeeling, that all human life is sacred and should be maintained, that suicide is wrong and euthanasia is too. Many felt that they could never comply with a loved one's wish to help them die. And since the laws in most of the country don't permit this, perhaps Mary was just spinning her wheels, striking listeners as either depressing or just boring in her seeming obsession with this issue.

But the seed leading to the letter continued to grow, deep within Mary. And this was an odd thing, because seeds are seen as the beginnings of life, as openings out into fullness, not into the arms of death. Finally, the day came, some months after the diagnosis of Alzheimer's that she'd so dreaded, and Mary was ready to write the letter. She feared further delay as her symptoms were increasing. This letter was an act that could profoundly shape the end of her life and the lives of those who loved her. She began, writing in longhand, so that she could feel the words forming on the paper.

"To my beloved husband and children: You are all well aware of my dismay at my father's long decline due to Alzheimer's, and of my fear that this will happen to me. And, to all of our sorrow, it now has. I want to prevent the long late stages of this terrible disease, and I hope that you will add this letter to my advance directives and follow it should the need arise, understanding that if I have lost my mind and will to act on my own behalf or ask assistance from others, your own help and support in ending my life will be a gift of love, one I will be able to count on when the dreadful shroud of dementia begins its slow, sorry smothering.

"If I remain conscious but have a progressive illness that will be fatal, and the illness is in an advanced stage, and I am consistently and permanently unable to communicate, to swallow food and water safely, to care for myself (including toileting) and to recognize my family and other people, and if substantial improvement of my condition is unlikely, I would like my wishes regarding specific life-sustaining treatments, as indicated in my advance directives, to be followed.

"In addition: If possible and if legal, I want to be given lethal drugs or an injection to swiftly and painlessly end my life. If this is still illegal, or not feasible, I do not want to be fed. I do not want to be given fluids. I want you to help me complete the process that will have already taken my humanity, my personhood. [This language is adapted from "The Dementia Provision" of the organization, Compassion and Choices; see below for further context.]

"Thank you, for your love and for all the ways your lives have enriched mine. I love you, and ask this out of love for you and love for myself. Yours, Mary."

Mary had then put down her pen. The sun's low, slanted beams heralded the coming autumn, but also filled her with hope that when the shadows began to fall for her, autumn would not last too long.

The lawyer now looked beseechingly at Jesus, still holding the letter.

"I know the law and I know the commandment to love God and neighbor and self. I do love God, and I love my wife, and, I suppose, myself as well. But my children and I are torn. We've read and talked about the letter, but now that it seems time to act, we don't know what to do. What is truly loving towards my wife, even towards those of us who have watched her decline into someone she would never want to be? Would assisting her death really be loving and not a sin? Or would it really be murder? And how should we pray? Where is God, and what is love, now—for Mary, and for us?

Jesus looked at the man, with all of the love of God in his eyes.

And Jesus wept.

Amen.

My sister, Christina, helped me further my thinking about the role of clergy, as she happened to be studying issues around medical ethics while I was working on this project. She pointed out that medicine is viewed more now as science than art, something that has not always been the case. And here I quote Christina: "Medicine, when considered as fact-based science, supported by quantifiable/verifiable evidence, seems to primarily guide life-end decisions, as opposed to religion, which is not based on quantifiable, verifiable facts. The process of dying, at least as it transpires in a hospital or institution, is medicalized, and priority is given to what can be quantified or expressed objectively, like heart rate, brain waves, and blood pressure versus an individual's wishes, which is a subjective condition, like 'quality of life,' 'dignity,' or 'personhood' (and includes adjectives like 'humiliating')."

Why should it be so much easier to ethically justify a decision that is tied to the objective markers of medicine than to the subjective ones of individual desire? I am trying to sort out here why the decision-making around death seems to be so skewed in the wrong direction! And why is medical involvement at the end of life so prevalent, especially once a person is terminally ill? I am not sure death should be so closely linked to medicine, as often, a medical/scientific solution is not possible, or even desired. But naturally, medicine is connected and rightly so, in those cases when medicine can prevent or delay an early, unwanted death. This makes it all the more difficult to try to extricate a medical approach to death from dementia-related and other special cases, because of its usefulness in so many circumstances. All the more reason for clergy to get more involved! Their voice in addressing these complicated moral issues is sorely needed.

Based on my feelings that clergy should become more involved in talking with their parishioners about end-of-life issues, I recently led a series of meetings, called "End of Life Conversations," at St. Columba's Episcopal Church in Washington, DC. Underpinning this work was my growing conviction that churches can do more than simply be available to visit the sick and dying and to help plan and lead funerals. Given the many questions around end-of-life situations, perhaps clergy can be more open to helping people face their questions and fears and hopes around dying. I was surprised at the response to the three-part series of ninety-minute sessions after church on Sunday. I expected eight to ten people, and only about that many actually responded to the announcement about the series. At the first session, twenty people showed up; at sessions two and three, there were thirty. And these really were conversations; I did not give talks to a passive audience. People were full of questions, eager to share their experiences. And there were many, so many tales of dementia and prolonged dying and not knowing what was possible and legal. These people very much wanted to talk about and actively explore end-of-life options but had rarely found opportunities to do this openly and in a safe place.

I learned from them, and they eagerly listened to quotations and poems and experiences I shared with them, including my own support for aid in dying, not only for those of sound mind but also for those with advanced dementia. There were some who wondered about the "playing God" question, and some who felt it would just be too hard to help another person die. When I held a later forum on funeral planning, called "Sacred Organizing," there was a similar response, with lots of people, lots of questions, and lots of gratitude that their church was offering resources to help them as they faced aging and eventual death.

I do feel that clergy have an important role to play in end-of-life care, and even if we do not all agree on issues of aid in dying, we can surely be open to our parishioners when they seek spiritual and practical guidance.

FIVE

Choices

We have one life to live and then we die. In contemporary terms, we die when the brain ceases to function. Both my wife and I have made our "final" wishes known in our end-of-life documents. In addition to the standard DNR (Do Not Resuscitate) order, we have provided that whenever we are in a terminal illness or there is an "irretrievable loss of personality," we authorize, in a Durable Power of Attorney given to each other and to our daughters, to "withhold nutrition and hydration" to allow our bodies to die.

From *The Jackdaw and the Peacock* by William A. Opel

Voluntary Stopping of Eating and Drinking (VSED)

Bill and Nina Opel have been friends of mine since 1975. He is a retired Episcopal priest and was an important mentor to me in the years when I was in seminary and moving toward ordination myself. Since then, the Opels have become dear friends, even though usually I see them only in the summer on Cape Cod. Bill had told me about his and Nina's advance directives before I ran across the above paragraph in Bill's book. It was not the first time I'd heard of such a plan.

Years earlier, I'd had lengthy conversations with a parishioner, Jerry, who also wanted to be able to stop eating and drinking in order to shorten his life. In Jerry's case, bone cancer was eating away at his body and the prospect of unbearable pain terrified him. He wanted to know if I thought it would be moral and legal for him to do this at home, and whether his wife would somehow be legally implicated if she cooperated. I did some research on pain management and finally talked to Dr. JoAnne Lynn (her real name, used by permission), then at Dartmouth College, about Jerry's case.

Dr. Lynn is now Director of the Altarum Center for Elder Care and Advanced Illness. She is a geriatrician, hospice physician, health services researcher, quality improvement advisor, and policy advocate. She has focused on shaping American health care so that every person can count on living comfortably and meaningfully through a period of serious illness and disability in the last years of life, at a sustainable cost to the community. At the time when I talked to her, she felt Jerry's desire to end his life by refusing nourishment was understandable and legitimate. She reminded me that when bodies are entering the terminal phase of a disease, they gradually shut down, and often the appetite for food lessens gradually, and, according to Dr. Lynn, hunger pangs are not severe. It is actually similar, she believes, to what happens with dying animals in the wild who often go off by themselves and stop foraging for food and drink. Jerry never needed to try his plan because a pain management crisis landed him in the hospital. But there, thanks to the ministrations of a caring nurse, he was given adequate morphine to control his pain, and perhaps, as is often the case with liberal morphine administration, it hastened his death.

From then on, I've been aware that stopping of eating and drinking is an option that would allow some autonomy for dying people, and that would be legal, if not in many institutions, at least in a private home. But Bill and Nina's plan is intended not only for a terminal illness, but also for an "irretrievable loss of personality," i.e., a situation of dementia.

However, with dementia, several questions and possible problems arise with the practice of what is now known by the name Voluntary Stopping of Eating and Drinking, and the acronym, VSED. At present, this practice appears to be the only possible legal way for people to help those who want to end their lives once dementia has robbed them so severely that they feel their lives are no longer worth prolonging. For mentally competent patients, like my friend Jerry, VSED could perhaps be done voluntarily, as was done in a much more recent and more public case, that of the well known radio talk show host, Diane Rehm, and her husband, John. John was in the late stages of Parkinson's disease when he asked to end his life through VSED and was able to do so with the help of his wife. Diane tells their story in her moving book, *On My Own*. Because John was of sound mind, he could express his wish to die in this way, and his wife and the facility where he lived were able to support him. His physician also provided guidance and help with managing what turned out to be a ten-day, gruelingly slow process of starvation.

For those with advanced dementia, however, the situation is different. Some cooperation would be needed from people who knew the wishes as expressed earlier by the patients, and are willing to honor them even if at the time VSED was carried out, they would have no way of knowing what the person wanted at that time—only what had been specified earlier, perhaps years earlier, and written down. With advanced dementia patients, the "voluntary" part of VSED becomes quite murky. How do such patients let us know what they actually want, and even if they could express themselves cogently, how should we weigh such wishes against what they clearly expressed before their disease took over?

The most helpful resource I've found about making a moral and legal case for VSED for patients with advanced dementia is an extraordinary article by Paul T. Menzel and Colette Chandler-Cramer in the 2014 May/June issue of "The Hastings Center Report." The article is entitled, "Advance Directives, Dementia, and Withholding Food and Water by Mouth." The following is drawn from that article.

Two main problems emerge in considering VSED for people with advanced dementia: The first is that the person with dementia may or may not be suffering, even if their condition meets the criteria they earlier specified as being intolerable to them. The second is about autonomy and whether the clearly expressed and written-down wishes of the person while of sound mind to end his life when dementia had reduced it to a certain degree could be considered valid in that later stage. Was the person really still the same person who had laid out the directives?

The authors make the case that advance directives to withhold food and water are already, if arguably, legal. They use three actual cases to present a sliding scale of situations in which VSED might be considered.

After Menzel and Chandler-Cramer discuss how late-stage dementia destroys the narrative of a person's life and takes away the legal options that competent patients have to control their ends of life, they examine the question of advance directives to withhold food and water by mouth at a certain point in advanced dementia. The authors argue that if advance directives have been established regarding withholding of nourishment, then honoring them is the same thing as honoring the expressed desire to withhold medical treatment, i.e., refusal of life support and refusal of food and water have equal legitimacy. So if it is legal for incompetent people to have advance directives refusing lifesaving, then it should be legal for them to have advance directives to suspend eating and drinking as well.

The authors consider in depth what they call the "then-self versus now-self." For them this "constitutes the most difficult and fundamental challenge to implementing any life-ending directive for people in dementia." If autonomy of the patient is to be respected, then how can that happen if the clearly stated wishes of the competent person are in direct conflict with what seem to be the wishes of the now severely demented person? The distinction here is between "critical and experiential interests." The former were those interests that were based on the values a person held while of sound mind and having true autonomy, on his sense of what made life important, what was crucial to the narrative of his life, and certainly on convictions about how his life should end. Experiential interests, such as hunger or fear or needs, like those of infants or very young children, can be quite different from one's critical interests, but the critical interests, expressed earlier, will still exist, even if the person no longer experiences them.

I might liken this distinction to that of a recovering alcoholic whose values have dictated that he abstains from alcohol (a critical interest) while his body and mind might occasionally cause him to desire to drink again (an experiential interest). We might agree that for this person the critical interest would take precedence. So based on this distinction, priority legally could be given to the interests expressed in an advance directive written when the patient still had full decisional capacity. Citing Ronald Dworkin, the authors claim that sacrificing one's critical interests to satisfy one's experiential interests would misconstrue one's best interests and would basically substitute the judgment of others for that of the patient. If critical interests represent what ultimately matters to a person, then they should have primacy, but only after a patient has really lost the capacity to value meaningful existence. The argument is that there must be a balancing of critical and experiential interests, and that this will change over time. It will thus be a subjective decision on the part of caregivers to withdraw nourishment, depending on what they deem the best interests of each patient, and this, I feel, will be one of the hardest sticking points in deciding when to honor advance directives for SED (Stopping Eating and Drinking).

Menzel and Chandler-Cramer lay out three somewhat different situations as a basis for looking at when and how VSED directives might be appropriately implemented.

The first would be when a patient who had very clear directives about VSED had reached the stage where her condition matched the criteria she had previously laid out. However, she could demonstrate that she still wanted to eat and drink, despite the directives, i.e., the then-self and the now-self are at odds. The authors suggest waiting, a "no, not yet" position on implementing the advance directive.

The second case arises when the person who wrote the directive actually resists eating and drinking, even if adequate assistance in doing so is offered. Menzel and Chandler-Cramer here feel that the now-self is aligned with the then-self; in neither case is eating or drinking desired, and so they should be stopped.

The most complicated situation occurs when the patient is indifferent to nourishment. She doesn't resist it, but does not indicate any desire for it. Here an alternative is suggested in the form of "Comfort Feeding Only" (CFO), which would lead eventually to death, but could be seen as a caring, respectful way of honoring directives. It might also prove more acceptable to caregivers who might be torn between the directives and their desire to deal in what they feel is a humane way with the demented person.

Having laid out three hypothetical situations, the authors proceed to justify two claims that they feel are necessary if advance directives for withholding food and water from a demented person are to be honored. The first is that this procedure is relatively comfortable; the second is that it is legal. They cite a variety of cases and studies that show VSED to actually offer a more comfortable and peaceful death than from other causes, but it is important that the methodology be tailored to produce this result. They point out that, at the time when SED directives would be initiated, the patient would likely already need a great deal of help with feeding, so that really it would be assistance rather than food and drink itself that would be withdrawn. This could perhaps be seen as analogous to failing to insert a feeding tube once a patient could not feed herself. It is also the case that many demented patients in advanced stages show few indications of hunger or thirst, so that for them, SED might be freer of discomfort than it would be for competent persons choosing VSED. The recommended process is to stop food first for one to three weeks and then withhold fluids. After two to four days, hunger pain mostly subsides, and the body further weakens (and some bodies are already very weak). Then with cessation of fluids, care is important to keep the lips and mouth from getting too dry. In the last two days or so, "patients often lapse into minimal consciousness, and some report euphoria near the end or earlier."

This description of how death comes so apparently benignly was surprising to me, but reassuring, compared to the way John Rehm's death was described. Other accounts—for instance, of death by starvation and dehydration among survivors of a shipwreck—are horrendous, but in those cases, no palliative care was available, and the sailors were also exposed to extremes of sun, heat, rain and cold. It does seem that effective education around VSED would be needed for both prospective patients and all caregivers, to reassure them that such a death would not be highly traumatic for anyone involved.

As mentioned above, the alternative procedure to SED or VSED that could lead gradually to death or to eventual SED is described as Comfort Feeding Only (CFO). After pointing out the drawbacks to feeding tubes, especially if there are advance directives asking for Stopping of Eating and Drinking, CFO is a sort of compromise. The patient is assisted with feeding only until they lose interest or indicate reluctance to eat. During the mealtime, other forms of comfort such as gently talking to or touching the patient are recommended as they provide caring interaction and would probably be more palatable to nursing home employees, even though this method would eventually lead to death. Although it seems CFO would not really honor specific advance directives about SED, it would come closer, and it would perhaps eventually lead to a more general acceptance of SED with adequate directives.

The second claim supported in the article is the one outlined above connecting the right to refuse medical treatment to the right to refuse nourishment. As both rights are available to a person of sound mind, the argument is that both should be available, based on clearly written advance directives, to those with dementia. However, as stated above, with dementia, the voluntary aspect may be missing, and what is really happening is SED by AD (Stopping of Eating and Drinking by Advance Directives). Because caregivers are involved in implementation, particularly in an institutional setting, there is the risk of being accused of neglect or abuse. In addition to very clear advance directives that clearly describe the situation in which SED would be desired, there would need to be "a reasonable interpretation of the now demented person's wishes and best interests (that) will support following the directive." An assurance that a care facility would not lose eligibility for Medicare and Medicaid if it honors such directives for SED also would be necessary, but the article's authors maintain that advance directives are a legal exception and that anyone who claims this concern as an excuse for refusing SED with AD is "speaking from ignorance." Finally, in terms of legality, carrying out the advance directive is something that caregivers can legally do, but they can't be obliged to do so.

The article concludes with a summary of the authors' position, which I quote here:

> Our position is moderate: implement a person's sufficiently clear AD to withhold food and water by mouth in severe dementia when implementation is justified by a diminished subjective value of survival that is outweighed by critical interests and autonomy...It is legally realistic in the entire United States, it is feasible within nursing home practice...and the deaths enabled by it can be comfortable.

What the authors point out as being so important are the huge benefits at stake for patients and families who are otherwise in the trap that advanced dementia lays: a person wishes to end his life should he become demented, but he cannot end his life because he has become demented.

At the time of this writing, only two legal remedies seem to be available for those who wish to avoid living through the late stages of dementia: pre-emptive suicide while the patient is still capable of that, and assisted SED according to very carefully prepared advance directives. In the latter case, both the legality of such a procedure, particularly in an institutional setting, and the assurance that the patient can be kept comfortable and peaceful as death arrives are essential. The family must check carefully with all caregivers, including each other, to ensure that they will comply with such directives. If not, the patient can be moved in order to carry them out.

In accordance with all of this thinking about legal options for end-of-life choices, one guide is "The Dementia Provision," which is published on the web site of the non-profit organization, Compassion & Choices, mentioned above. This seems a bit surprising as the organization states in its Spring 2018 magazine that Compassion & Choices does not support access to medical aid in dying, but for some, the distinction between this and SED with advance directives, such as given in the provision below, will be crucial.

Dementia Clauses in Advance Directives

Most Advance Directives become operative only when a person is unable to make health care decisions and is either "permanently unconscious" or "terminally ill." There is usually no provision that applies to the situation in which a person suffers from severe dementia, but is neither unconscious nor dying.

The following language can be added to any Advance Directive or Living Will. There, it will serve to advise physicians and family of the wishes of a patient with Alzheimer's Disease or other form of dementia. You may simply sign and date this form and include it with the form "My Particular Wishes" in your Advance Directive:

If I am unconscious and it is unlikely that I will ever become conscious again, I would like my wishes regarding specific life-sustaining treatments, as indicated on the attached document, entitled "My Particular Wishes," to be followed.

If I remain conscious but have a progressive illness that will be fatal and the illness is in an advanced stage, and I am consistently and permanently unable to communicate, swallow food and water safely, care for myself and recognize my family and other people, and it is very unlikely that my condition will substantially improve, I would like my wishes regarding specific life-sustaining treatments, as indicated on the attached document, entitled "My Particular Wishes," to be followed.

If I am unable to feed myself while in this condition:
I do / do not (circle one) want to be fed.
I do / do not (circle one) want to be given fluids.

I hereby incorporate this provision into my durable power of attorney for health care, living will, and any other previously executed advance directive for health care decisions.

Signature and Date

The Dementia Provision, 10/2014

Another example of a dementia-specific Advance Directive is a draft from Terry Dowd, a parishioner at St. Columba's Church in Washington, DC:

Directions to my health care [agent/proxy] about ending my life in the event that I cannot make decisions:

NAME:

My values and wishes:

If I contract dementia, Alzheimer's, or other progressive brain disease, I do not wish to prolong my life, once the conditions set below are met:

I do not want to burden my [wife/husband/partner] or other members of my family emotionally and physically during a prolonged period. I do not want my illness to become a financial burden and drain resources, either my own, my family's, the government's or any other provider's.

These are the conditions under which I do not want to prolong my life and wish to die:

I am unresponsive to my environment and this is unlikely to change.

I am unresponsive to my [wife/husband/partner] and other loved ones and this is unlikely to change.

"Unresponsive" means that most of the time I am unaware, do not communicate effectively, do not remember, and do not understand.

When my health care [agent/ proxy] decides [*optional*: after consultation with my physician] that these conditions are met, I request that my health care [agent/ proxy] make the following decisions on my behalf and ensure that they are carried out:

• All food should be discontinued by whatever means administered. I do not want to be served food or to be giving assistance in taking in food.

• All fluids should be discontinued. I do not want fluids served to me or to be given assistance in drinking fluids. Appropriate means to reduce dry mouth are acceptable.

• All medications and therapies that I take or use should be discontinued, unless they are considered a matter of comfort.

• Any medications should be administered that will help my death be as peaceful as possible.

To those whom I am trusting to carry out my wishes, I understand that taking these steps will be difficult for you. I hope that you will be able to do it, knowing that this is what I want for my sake and yours.

[*Optional*: I am not afraid of dying and of dying in this manner. I love you.]

Signature:_____

Date:_____

Witness signature:_____

Date:_____

Witness name printed: _____

Witness address:_____

Witness signature:_____

Date:_____

Witness name printed:_____

Witness address:_____

SIX

A Different Story of Dad

I have recounted above in the third chapter, "The Story of Dad," my Dad's early symptoms and then his diagnosis and eventual move to a nursing home once it was no longer feasible for my mother to care for him at home. I've described what happened over the four years there as his worst fears about losing his mind were realized. And how he finally died. Now I offer an alternative scenario, one that would have honored my father's expressed desire to not go on living should he lose his mind.

After the Alzheimer's diagnosis, as oldest daughter, and as a minister with some experience of people at various stages of dementia, I ask for and plan a meeting with my parents and all five of us siblings to talk frankly about the diagnosis and how this disease will likely play out. Before the meeting, I ask that we all inform ourselves thoroughly about Alzheimer's so that we will have enough information to realistically assess options for Dad's care. It feels almost like planning an intervention for an alcoholic, with all the uncertainty about how people will respond and whether they will be offended or angered if the subject of assisted suicide comes up. Maybe denial will be the preferred coping mode, with people saying, "It's way too soon to be talking about all this. Dad is pretty much fine now—aren't you, Dad?" Maybe Mom will be horrified and say something like, "It don't believe in suicide; I think it's a sin!"

For my own preparation, I read my way through the chapter on Alzheimer's in Sherwin Nuland's book, *How We Die*, a brave, raw look at what this relentless dementia does to people and to the families and others who care for them. I would also have tackled all three-hundred-plus pages of *The 36-Hour Day* by Nancy Mace and Peter Rabins, the comprehensive go-to tome for people caring for victims of dementia. In reading both of these books, I am shocked to find that nowhere was the possibility of assisted suicide for dementia ever raised! As if no one would have ever considered this?

I prepare my case to make to the family, including the toll we will see on our beloved father and husband, but also on each of us as his deterioration drags on with no end in sight. I plan to use quotes from Nuland, such as the following:

"There is no dignity in this kind of death" (117).

"Alzheimer's is one of those cataclysms that seems designed specifically to test the human spirit...The cost, of course is considerable. In terms of emotional damage, of neglect of personal goals and responsibilities, of disturbed relationships, and of financial resources, the toll is unbearably high. Few tragedies are more expensive" (105).

Fortunately, my siblings and my mother and father all agree to the meeting. We begin by telling Dad how much we love him, what a great father and husband he has been, and how now, with this diagnosis, we need to talk about the future. We want to explore ways in which we can honor whatever his best hopes and wishes are for the rest of his life. We share what we know of the disease, remembering a neighbor who had it, and how we had watched him worsen until he was moved to a nursing home where he died years later. Some of us feel that somehow it will be different for Dad, or at least that's our hope.

"That was Ken," says our brother, Bob. "Dad would never turn out like that!"

"I think your Dad can try much harder to remember stuff and not to repeat questions," says Mom. "Maybe the medications he's been prescribed will help."

Others of us chime in, almost in unison, "We want you to be able to stay at home!"

Dad echoes that. "Don't put me away in one of those places; I'd rather die."

Finally, I venture forth with my memory of what Dad said years ago about not wanting to be kept alive if he lost his mind. Dad remembers!

"I did say that, didn't I?"

But of course, we all rush to insist that we're not there yet. Dad is far from that place; his life is still good.

But the specter looms, and we all know it. He will lose his mind. It may be two years, it may be five or ten, but the time will come when the person he is now will be gone, and what will be left is not anyone he would ever want to be. His intelligence, his dignity, his capacity to know and love all of us will be gone. This is what he meant—he will not want to be alive when that time comes. He will not want to have to live through it, and he will not want the rest of us to go through it either. All of this is unspoken, but I think Dad is still cognizant of it. And I'm sure he also realizes that taking care of him for however many years will cost a tremendous amount of money—money he has earned and preserved for his own and our mother's old age, and he's not sure it will last if he has to spend years in a nursing home.

"So, Dad," I ask, "are you saying you want to end your own life at some point, or that you want us to help?" We are quiet, not sure what we want to hear.

In as lucid a tone as any he's ever had, Dad speaks.

"I hope that when this thing has really got me, when I don't know who you are, when I can't speak, have to wear diapers and be fed like a baby, when all I can do is sit and look stupid, I hope then, one of you will help me take some medicine that will kill me. I don't know what will be legal then, but I hope there's a way. I'll be too far gone to plan and do it myself, or I would." And then Dad adds: "I've written down what I want. I knew I had to do it while I still could. You can find my directive attached to my will in that file, and I hope, when the time comes, you'll understand and help me. I want this, not just for myself, but because I love you all and want the best for you."

We are shocked at his clarity. It's as though he's been thinking this through since he first began to have symptoms and was just waiting for someone to ask him about the end. And we know this conversation is important now, because later, Dad will be too impaired to have it. I am flooded with feelings of love and respect for this man who is facing what for him is the worst way to die. I am glad he wants to wait until he is truly no longer himself, and that he is not (apparently) planning to commit suicide on his own anytime soon when he would still be mentally capable of planning and carrying it out. He does want more time with us; he wants all the good time he can get. But then he asks our help in bringing about a swift, painless death, in which Alzheimer's is robbed of its victory, so that he, and we, would find relief.

I am once again moved, even to tears, to hear my own father lay out what he has been thinking. Before long, I'll no longer have access to that; and so this conversation and what Dad has put in writing is a gift. We won't have to struggle to know what he thinks or wants. We won't have to all be guessing and speculating about what is going on inside him, about who, in fact, he really is, and how he would want to be cared for.

"But what if it's illegal?" says our mother. "And furthermore, I could never give you those pills."

"Me, neither," says Bob.

"I could, in a heartbeat," says our sister, Christina.

Brother Tom, in his measured way of speaking says, "Dad, I could take you to Oregon, where assisted suicide is legal, and help you there when the time comes."

Clearly, we're not all in agreement, but at least we've heard from Dad, and we'll have this gathering to remember and refer to when it comes time to make difficult decisions.

After that amazingly candid conversation, our spirits are lifted, and we face the next days and months of life with Dad with a sense of sadness, but also a sense of ease. We have not yet worked out for ourselves what to do, or the legal ramifications of helping Dad, but we are not plagued with the helplessness of watching all of our worst expectations inexorably come about.

I then get in touch with Compassion & Choices, the organization that not only offers support to people who want to end their lives when facing terminal illness, but that also lobbies to change laws, state by state, to allow for assisted suicide. They confirm that, at present, all such laws include only those who are of sound mind when they ask for help in ending their lives. The kind and perceptive woman I speak with on the phone understands well the dilemma here. Dementia patients are facing a horrific dying process in terms of length, loss of dignity and quality of life, and yet they are excluded from the merciful treatment afforded to others who wish to end their lives. She noted that some patients may choose to end their lives before the disease truly ravages their minds because once it has, they know they will be incapable of expressing the wish or planning a way to end their lives on their own.

She tells me that Compassion and Choices offers a sample Dementia Clause that can be added to one's advance directives and living will. We get a copy and ask Dad if he wants to do this, and he signs it with a still steady hand. But he also adds that he'd prefer to be given lethal medication, which would be quicker and painless, and we all hope that will be legal by the time we need it.

Life with Dad becomes more and more difficult. He exhausts Mom by asking her the same questions over and over: "Are we having lunch soon?" having just finished it. "Where are we going?" after being told five times. There is occasional incontinence—not a huge problem at home, but excruciatingly embarrassing in a public place. He goes off on walks, and we fear he'll cause an accident or become lost. He shows no interest in reading or crossword puzzles, and he becomes more and more quiet, talking little, and then mostly only to Mom, asking her questions when we're not around. He seems to be trying to hide his impairment from everyone else.

On the other hand, he can be sweet, child-like and loving. I show him family photo albums, and although he doesn't seem to recognize anyone, he seems engaged and glad to look at the pictures. Same with simple toys: a frog that lights up and opens his mouth when you push a button. And music still works. He recognizes a few familiar songs, like his college *Alma Mater*, and he can even remember words and sing along. He loves to eat, and going out for dinner can be fun if the restaurant is simple and service is quick; otherwise, he loses track of whether we've been served or not, and gets impatient. He still loves ice cream, and as he is no longer concerned about gaining weight, which he always was before, he puts on pounds.

All five of us children take turns visiting and giving our mother a break, but the brunt of the support falls to our younger sister, Christina, who lives thirty minutes away, and who puts in many hours running errands, spending time with Dad, and helping our mother.

However, as the months stretch on, we begin to realize that this situation will not last. We are losing Dad, or at least "the Dad that was," as we refer to our father before Alzheimer's.

It's now time for another meeting, including Dad. None of us feel that he is ready to give up his life, and he agrees. But Mom can't really care for him any more on her own, and she also feels he can't be left alone in the apartment. We all agree, however, that we don't want to move him to a care facility. In the back of our minds, we know that once there, it would be almost impossible to help him die, and he'd really be trapped in the exact scenario he has clearly said he doesn't want. It seems that home health care of some sort is our best option.

Within days we have located an experienced home health aide who will come on weekdays to provide help and respite care for

Mom. Dad actually likes this woman and the attention she gives him, even accompanying him on walks around the neighborhood. Mom gets out more to play bridge and see friends, and all of us take turns visiting more frequently. A semblance of order is restored, and although the real Dad is no longer with us, a still handsome if slightly dilapidated looking Dad greets us vaguely, and seems content with his days of simple needs met and childlike pleasures of toys and pictures and music, and non-conversations. I always tell him who I am, but I don't think it registers. I think he just knows someone is there who feels familiar. I'm not even sure he knows Mom. Sometimes he calls her "Jane," his deceased sister's name.

As the months go on, I am filled with foreboding. Now Alzheimer's is really annihilating the Dad that was, to a point where we must face his stated desire to stop living. Bob thinks he has good days and isn't ready; Mom insists she can't be part of it; the other four of us siblings think the time is coming soon. Dad no longer knows any of us. He barely speaks, and when he does, he is usually incoherent. The health aide manages diapering and bathing and physical care, but the loss of control of bodily functions and of the dignity Dad once had would have been harrowing for the Dad that was, a very private and modest man in these personal matters.

I call our local primary care doctor, Sid, with whom we've all been in conversation over the past couple of years. Although, legally, he can in no way participate in assisted suicide or euthanasia, he is extremely sympathetic to this situation, which he has faced countless times; he has indicated that he can enable us to get prescription drugs that will end our father's life or, if we so choose, that he will support us in withholding food and drink from Dad in order to bring about his death.

He comes over to the apartment for a visit with us and with Dad, who of course has no idea who he is. Sid jokes with him, saying, "Are you the lucky guy?" and observes for a while, sadness creasing his usually jovial expression. "Bob was a dear friend," he says, "smart, funny, a real contributor to this community. I know he would hate what has become of him, and I respect your desire to honor his wishes." He gives us a prescription.

Dad's eighty-sixth birthday is approaching—January 7, 2004. He is no longer part of our conversations, even if he's in the room with us. It is clear he is not only not "the Dad that was," but that he has lost almost all of what makes us human—the ability to communicate, to express and receive love, to think or imagine or remember. His body looks tired and thin, and his eyes look vacant. He is no longer here, nor would he want to be. And so we agree, not easily, but eventually, that his birthday would be a good day, ending his life on the same date as it began.

January 7 is very cold, but clear and crisp. All five of us children have arrived in the past couple of days, two of us from Washington, DC, and the others from Providence, Rhode Island, Ithaca, New York, and across town in Pittsburgh. It feels too private to bring our spouses or children; we want only our nuclear family as we were, growing up. We have talked of how it should go. We want to have music playing. Dad had said Rachmaninoff's Piano Concerto No. 2 was his favorite piece of music, and that won the day over the Cornell *Alma Mater*. We gather in the apartment in late afternoon, dressed casually but somberly, except Mom, who dresses up in a beautiful sweater and skirt and some favorite jewelry Dad gave her. Bob's wife has sent a gorgeous bouquet of peach and white and lavender flowers, a hint of spring. The caregiver has gone home early. Dad is in his bed, dressed in clean blue pajamas, sitting up against pillows. We could all use something to drink, and so we open a good bottle of wine and make cocktails for those who prefer. That includes Dad, for whom we pour out his last gin and tonic. Brother Tom lifts a glass of ginger ale.

Now we're not quite sure what to do. I've thought all along that as the oldest child and then the first to hear Dad express his wish that he not go on living should he lose his mind, I should be the one to give him the pills that end his life. I should be the one to kill our father—what an extraordinary presumption! How can we do this, and how can I be the agent? These feelings are rushing and swirling in me, but they are met with other feelings, even more insistent. I love Dad with all my heart, and I want to do what he said he wanted; I want to end what for him loomed as torture and is now playing out against his will. I will act in mercy and love and compassion, and I will make happen the thing we have all agreed upon, the thing Dad asked.

I am stirring the pills into a plain glass of Coke, no ice (that's how Dad always ordered it) as my head and my heart spin with a sense of something portentous, irrevocable. I am ending the life of the one who gave me life. Or no, I am ending the slow, demeaning dying of a man whose real life is already over. Realizing that no one is saying anything, I look around.

"It's OK, Sue, go ahead," says Bob.

"You can do this," says Marty, and Tom chokes out, "I love you, Dad."

Christina has her arms around Mom, who is crying, and has been the most ambivalent. But then Mom moves close to Dad and bravely takes his hand. Christina looks at me and says, "Please."

I offer Dad the glass and he begins to drink it down. We are transfixed, holding our breaths, hardly able to look. One by one, each of us says, as if we'd rehearsed it, "I love you, Dad. Good-bye."

And then, just as the doctor promised, Dad closes his eyes and lies back on the pillows. He looks peaceful. He makes no sound, and within a few minutes, he is still, and seemingly unconscious. Marty, a nurse, begins to check his pulse as we wait, almost paralyzed, for Dad to stop breathing. After about a half an hour, he does. We touch him, we hug each other, we cry, more from relief than sadness. We begin to make all the arrangements that come with a death, any death, but this one has been chosen, and welcome—our last best gift to this man we've all loved for so long.

AFTERWORD

A Long Term Goal—or Just a Dream

I have navigated in these pages the long and winding paths of those who have confronted death at the end of the tunnel that is dementia. I've seen those who decided to end their own lives while of sound mind in order to control the circumstances of their deaths. I've looked at what is possible now, legally, for those who want to avoid late-stage dementia. Those options seem to be only two: pre-emptive suicide while they still have the capacity to carry it out, and voluntary stopping of eating and drinking, according to detailed advance directives honored and supported by family and caregivers. Both have serious drawbacks, but may still be deemed better than the alternative of letting Alzheimer's take its course.

The first option has the obvious cost of shortening one's life prematurely, thus losing what could be several years of enjoyment, perhaps the pleasures of being with spouse, children and friends, of watching grandchildren grow, being outdoors, reading, watching movies and TV, listening to music, pursuing hobbies, loving pets, savoring good food. A pre-emptive suicide seems a denial of the preciousness of life, and maybe an unneeded sacrifice before that life had been irredeemably depleted.

Another cost would be its impact on others. A spouse, other family members and friends might feel robbed, plunged into premature grief if early dementia hadn't yet seemed too much of a problem. The afflicted person might decide to be open about her plans and try to convince others to support her, thus risking their opposition and perhaps strict measures to prevent her. Or she could act in secret, perhaps adding a sense of betrayal to a family's loss and grief: "Why didn't she tell us; how could she leave us too soon?"

Finally, the practical matter of carrying out a pre-emptive suicide could be difficult. One would need access to an effective weapon or lethal medication and the ability to use it. Our lax gun laws would probably help there, or a person could opt for hanging or other forms of suicide. One might be able to find a sympathetic physician to write a prescription, but that person would be taking an ethical risk unless an aid-in-dying law was in effect. Even then, there would be a question about the person's full mental capacity and the problem of not being within six months of death as most such laws stipulate. With any suicide attempt, there is the risk of a botched attempt leading to further impairment, and again, the distress of the family struggling to understand such desperation. And, except for death by lethal medication, which would act swiftly and painlessly, most suicides are violent, even painful deaths, probably carried out alone, ugly and shocking to come upon.

The second, at least theoretically legal option for avoiding late-stage dementia, VSED (really SED, as the voluntary factor would be gone) has been described in depth in the chapter on that topic. Assuming advance directives were carefully and thoroughly written, and family and institutional caregivers were willing to co-operate, this could certainly shorten the lives of dementia patients and provide them with some control over the endings of their lives. One difficulty would be determining at what point to begin withholding nourishment. Even with crystal clear directives, uncertainty could arise because various limitations would come about sporadically. A patient might fail to recognize anyone for several weeks and then have a moment or a day of clarity, might remain mute for days and then utter a sentence or sing a fragment of song. It could be a very hard call to know exactly when the conditions spelled out in the directives for SED were in place, and there could be disagreements among family members or with caregivers.

Above and beyond this difficulty is one I find much more serious, which is that stopping nutrition, and especially liquids, leads to a slow death, not a quick and painless and peaceful one. Despite accounts of hunger pains and thirst diminishing after a day or two, and the body gradually shutting down, and the role of sedation and comfort care, this is still a process that can take up to a couple of weeks. Because of the loss of mental competence and comprehension, the patient may feel terribly confused, neglected, and even uncomfortable, but have no way of expressing that, even if the process is something she originally specified in her directives. Watching a loved one starve to death could be a grueling process for all involved, again, even if they knew it was what the patient had wanted. The goal—release from the even longer end stage of Alzheimer's—might be worth it, but SED, in my view, is an unnecessarily onerous way to have to get there.

I have come to a pause, a stumbling block, really, as I press into my quest to allow for aid in dying for advanced dementia patients. I have always wanted to be open-minded about the various options available to these patients and their caregivers, and I'm trying to resist advocating any one path as the right one. Dementia is too devastating, too various in its manifestations and meandering progress. There are indeed serious moral questions around any decision to take a life or help someone to do so, even if that is their wish. Aid in dying is only one option, and I realize that for many, it is simply out of the question.

But for those who would choose aid in dying, there is an issue of fairness. If aid in dying in the form of lethal medications is available in an increasing number of states to persons of sound mind, then that equal treatment should be available to dementia patients as long as their request for this aid has been made while still mentally, and thus legally, capable. It is hard enough for someone to face the gradual erosion of his personhood, hard enough for all who love him to stand by as it happens. Why should the only legal (and even this is debatable) remedy be so much more onerous on all concerned than the ingestion of a pill that would act swiftly and painlessly? Shouldn't advanced dementia patients have an equal opportunity under the law to choose to shorten their dying process?

This opportunity may be a long time in coming, but it is my fervent hope that as aid-in-dying laws are passed in more and more states, they will include provisions for dementia patients. Concerns about such patients being pressured to write such directives or to have them carried out, especially for financial reasons, are real. These are slippery slope arguments, however, and needn't block the inclusion of dementia as a terminal illness warranting death-with-dignity options.

Life is indeed sacred, and choices about ending it are intensely personal, and sacred as well. No one should ever be coerced; no one should ever be forced to write directives asking for aid in dying; no doctor should ever be forced to provide it. In this sense it is like abortion—a choice that people are free to make, but a choice they are free to completely reject. We are each different, and each of us will face the end of this life in our own way. It is my strong hope and longing that when that time comes for me and for all those whom I love, if dementia is part of that story, we will have the freedom to choose an end that is consistent with our most deeply cherished values and the love and support of those around us to honor that choice. I wish my father had had that, and I hope his story and its impact on me will one day help make this possible for others.

ACKNOWLEDGEMENTS

This book has taken me a very long time to write and an even longer time germinating in my heart and soul. Along the way I have been helped and encouraged especially by my siblings, Marty Mann, Bob Mann, Tommie Mann and Christina Schmidlapp, who shared my anguish as we gradually lost our father to dementia. Parishioners of three Episcopal churches have listened to me preach about or discuss aid in dying: St. Mark's, Capitol Hill and St. Columba's in Washington, DC and St. John's Norwood in Chevy Chase, MD. They, along with a number of other clergy colleagues, were most helpful with their feedback and questions. Their willingness to address this subject confirmed my sense that dementia is a spiritual issue, a spiritual loss, and that aid in dying is indeed an appropriate topic for faith communities to engage. Numerous books and more articles than I could possibly list, only some of which are included the Bibliography, have informed my thinking and made me realize the timeliness and importance of aid in dying for dementia patients.

In the writing itself, my memoir group, led by Sara Tabor, was a monthly blessing over several years. Irene Landsman, Taisie Berkeley, Christie Platt, Peggy Treadwell, and Ann Varnon were faithful and insightful critics as this project took shape. They kept urging me on with their sense that the special cases of dementia patients need to be considered as our culture becomes more accepting of aid in dying. My stepdaughter, Lili Flanders, a published writer herself, provided steady encouragement when this project faltered, and was particularly helpful in discussing dementia provisions and how they might be drafted and discussed in families. Tucker Clark, an experienced editor, was enormously helpful in an initial overall review including key comments, questions and corrections. I particularly thank Rhonda Shary for the final detailed editing and critique. Her work was painstaking and caring and greatly strengthened the text. Haley Chung of Opus Press deftly guided me through the whole publication process. My husband, Bill, besides lending careful attention to the chapter on his own father's Alzheimer's, has been patient and loving throughout, and I love him for his careful inquiries and constant support.

Finally, this book is the story not only of my father, but of all of the others whose stories have helped me to understand the dilemma that dementia poses for those who would seek aid in dying, but are at present unable to do so. These patients and their families have made it possible to raise the questions, consider various arguments, offer some answers, and finally to advocate for the option of aid in dying for this growing segment of our population. Their stories form the heart of this book, and though mostly unnamed within, they will know who they are. They have my gratitude and love.

Bibliography

American Heritage Dictionary of the English Language, Fifth ed.
    "Euthanasia." New York: Houghton Mifflin Harcourt,
    2015.

Bailey, Melissa. "Billions Spent, But a Cure for Alzheimer's Remains
    Elusive." *The Sydney (Australia) Morning Herald.* February
    7, 2017. https://www.smh.com.au/business/billions-spent-but
    a-cure-for-alzheimers-remains-elusive-20170207-
    gu6wjx.html (accessed August 10, 2018).

Carter, Zoe Fitzgerald. *Imperfect Endings: A Daughter's Story of Love,
    Loss, and Letting Go.* New York: Simon & Schuster,   2011.

Comer, Meryl. *Slow Dancing with a Stranger.* New York: Harper
    One-Harper Collins, 2014.

Dworkin, Ronald. "On Autonomy and the Demented Self." Oxford
    and New York: *Milbank Quarterly* 64 (February 1986): 4-16.
    Quoted in Atul Gawande. *Being Mortal.*

Flamm, Hannah. "Why Are Nursing Homes Drugging
Dementia Patients Without Their Consent?" *The
Washington Post*, August 10, 2018.

Gawande, Atul. *Being Mortal: Medicine and What Matters in the End.*
New York: Metropolitan Books-Henry Holt &
Company, 2014.

Genova, Lisa. *Still Alice*. iUniverse, 2007. New York: Pocket Books-
Simon & Schuster, 2009.

*The New Oxford Annotated Bible, third Edition, New Revised Standard
Version*. Oxford University Press, 2001

Fox, Zach. "Boiling Springs Man Pleads Guilty in 'Merciful' Killing of
Parents." *Goupstate.com*. January 4, 2018. Updated 5, 2018.
http://www.goupstate.com/news/20180104/boiling-springs-
man-pleads-guilty-in-merciful-killing-of-parents (accessed
August 6, 2018).

Lamott, Anne. *Grace (Eventually): Thoughts on Faith*. New York:
Riverhead, 2007.

Mace, Nancy and Peter Rabins. *The 36-Hour Day: A Family Guide to
Caring for People Who Have Alzheimer Disease, Related*

Dementias, and Memory Loss. Baltimore: Johns Hopkins University Press, 2012.

Menzel, Paul T. and Colette Chandler-Cramer. "Advance Directives, Dementia, and Withholding Food and Water by Mouth." *The Hastings Center Report* 44 (3) (May/June 2014): 23-47.

Merriam-Webster Ninth New Collegiate Dictionary. "Suicide." New York: Merriam Webster, 1990.

Merriam-Webster.com. "Assisted suicide." https://www.merriam-webster.com/dictionary/physician-assisted%20suicide (accessed August 10, 2018). ---. "Physician-assisted suicide."

Nuland, Sherwin. *How We Die: Reflections on Life's Final Chapter*. New York: Penguin Random House, 1994.

One True Thing. Directed by Carl Franklin. Screenplay by Karen Croner. Performers, Meryl Streep, Renee Zellwegger, and William Hurt. USA: Monarch Pictures, Universal Pictures, 1998.

Opel, William A. *The Jackdaw and the Peacock: Biblical Mistranslations and Christian Traditions*. Haworth, NJ: St. Johann Press, 2014.

Quindlen, Anna. *One True Thing*. New York: Random House, 1994.

Rehm, Diane. *On My Own*. New York: Alfred A. Knopf, 2016.

Seneca the Elder. Quoted in *The History of European Morals from Augustus to Charlemagne, Volume I*, William Edward Hartpole Lecky 1869. Quoted in Sherwin Nuland. *How We Die.*

Still Alice. Directed and Written by Richard Glatzer, Wash Westmoreland. Performers, Julianne Moore, Alec Baldwin, and Kristen Stewart. USA, UK and France: BSM Studio, Big Indie Films, Shriver Films, 2014. Distributed by Sony Pictures Classics, 2014.

Will, George F. "Affirming a Right to Die with Dignity." *The Washington Post*, August 28, 2015. https://www.washingtonpost.com/opinions/distinctions-in-end-of-life-decisions/2015/08/28/b34b8f6a-4ce7-11e5-902f39e9219e574b_story.html?utm_term=.2ae2a256d221 (accessed July 31, 2018).

CPSIA information can be obtained
at www.ICGtesting.com
Printed in the USA
FFHW02n1649191018
48893059-53110FF

9 781624 291852